COLLOQUIAL
ENGLISH

THE COLLOQUIAL SERIES

*Colloquial Albanian
*Colloquial Arabic of Egypt
*Colloquial Arabic (Levantine)
*Colloquial Arabic of the Gulf and Saudi Arabia
*Colloquial Chinese
*Colloquial Czech
Colloquial Dutch
*Colloquial English
*Colloquial French
Colloquial German
Colloquial Greek
*Colloquial Hungarian
*Colloquial Italian
*Colloquial Japanese
*Colloquial Persian
*Colloquial Polish
Colloquial Portuguese
*Colloquial Romanian
Colloquial Russian
*Colloquial Serbo-Croat
Colloquial Spanish
*Colloquial Swedish
*Colloquial Turkish

*Accompanying cassette available

COLLOQUIAL ENGLISH

Graham Coe

London and New York

To Joan

First published in 1981
by Routledge & Kegan Paul Ltd
Reprinted in 1982, 1986 and 1987
Reprinted in 1989 (twice) and 1992
by Routledge
11 New Fetter Lane, London EC4P 4EE

Simultaneously published in the USA and Canada
by Routledge
a division of Routledge, Chapman and Hall, Inc.
29 West 35th Street, New York, NY 10001

© Graham Coe 1981
Set in 9/11 Linoterm Times by
Rowland Phototypesetting, Bury St Edmunds, Suffolk
Printed and bound in Great Britain by
Cox & Wyman Ltd, Reading

All rights reserved. No part of this book may be reprinted or reproduced or utilized in any form or by any electronic, mechanical, or other means, now known or hereafter invented, including photocopying and recording, or in any information storage or retrieval system, without permission in writing from the publishers.

British Library Cataloguing in Publication Data

Coe, Graham
Colloquial English.–(Routledge colloquial series).
1. English language – Text-books for foreigners
2. English language – Spoken English
I. Title
428.2'4   PE1128   80-41795

ISBN 0-415-02769-1
ISBN 0-415-04567-3 (cassette)

CONTENTS

ACKNOWLEDGMENTS vii
INTRODUCTION ix
FOR THE TEACHER xi

1 I'd like to book a flight. 1
2 Which way do I go now? 10
3 They're asking us to fasten our seat belts. 21
4 I hope we haven't missed our connection. 32
5 Can you find out how to turn the water on? 43
6 It says they've got boats for hire. 54
7 I couldn't drink any more, thanks. 65
8 We'd better look at the map again. 75
9 Can I have one made to measure? 85
10 We could see them doing the flower dance. 96
11 She seems to be the best qualified. 106
12 You're supposed to insert a twenty-cent coin. 117
13 Keep gargling with warm salt water. 128
14 They should've used more waterproof paper. 140
15 The damage can't be too serious. 150
16 There must be someone under that floor. 162
17 It's time we cut the tape. 172
18 Is everyone in favour? 186

KEY TO PRACTICE EXERCISES 198
ACTIVITIES INDEX 226
IMPORTANT WORDS: A CHECK-LIST 228

ACKNOWLEDGMENTS

The author and publishers are grateful to the following for permission to reproduce copyright material:

London Transport Ltd for the map of the London Underground and material adapted from the pamphlet 'Underground to Heathrow' (pp. 16–19);
The Consumers Association for illustrations and material adapted from the July 1977 issue of *Which?* (p. 93);
The Post Office for information taken from the Telephone Directory (pp. 122–4).

INTRODUCTION

The aim of this book is to help the student of English as a foreign or second language to use colloquial English. It is for learners anywhere in the world who have completed about three years of English at secondary level (whether recently or some time ago) and who need to revise and improve their speaking and understanding of English for social purposes or for their work.

The book is divided into 18 Units, graded in order of difficulty. Each Unit is built around six or seven short dialogues in which essential functions of colloquial English are practised. Examples of printed material illustrating various uses of English, together with sketches and diagrams, help to reinforce the language in the dialogues. There are numerous practice exercises, some of which need answers. You can check the answers from the Key at the back of the book. Also at the back of the book is a check-list of important words used in the book (the words in the 'boxes') and a list of the main activities around which it is written. There is also a cassette recording of the dialogues. This is an essential part of the course.

If necessary the student can use this book without a teacher, though obviously it is useful to have at least the help of a friend to converse with. For each Unit, read the introduction to the dialogues first. Then read the dialogues (you will need a good dictionary to help you with unfamiliar vocabulary). Listen to the dialogues, then listen to them again, making pauses for repetition. Repeat after each speaker or in the middle of longer sentences. Do this several times. It is a good idea to learn bits of the dialogues by heart. When you know the dialogues well do the practice work (remember this is designed for self-help) and the rest of the work in the Unit. A lot of the practice work, including the comprehension questions, should be done in writing. Choose your answers as far as possible from the dialogues or other material in the same Unit. Check your answers from the Key. But please note that in many exercises various answers are possible. Only one answer is given in the Key – the answer which is closest to the language in that Unit.

Some practice is given in listening for the changes of tone in certain phrases or sentences. This helps the student to realise that intonation in English helps us to express meaning.

For teachers who are going to use this book with their students there follow some further brief notes.

Meanwhile, welcome to Arcania, where most of the action in this book takes place.

FOR THE TEACHER

This book spans the intermediate learning stage, from low to high intermediate. It seeks to reinforce and enrich language skills that have probably been neglected, due to the requirements of many a formal English syllabus. It is designed to be of use in any country in the world and will prove especially useful for students in language schools. It is suited for use on a self-help basis which is why more of the mechanical type of exercises are present in the book. But a teacher's guidance and encouragement are, of course, always beneficial.

The dialogues and practice sections have been specially written. They may be regarded as reconstructions of spoken language, edited for the printed page. The material for Further Study has been adapted from typical examples of written English (notices, guidebooks, etc).

While exposing the student to a wide range of colloquial English forms and styles we have naturally had to limit the selection of items to be taught. It is not possible to encompass the whole range of colloquial English patterns and idioms in a short book of this kind. Therefore you should regard this course as a stimulus for developing colloquial skills which can then be used in an infinite number of more specialised activities. Within the functional framework which is linked together (not too tightly) by the events in the book there has been a tacit grading of structural patterns, based on the schedule presented in 'English Grammatical Structure' by L. G. Alexander and others (published by Longman). But it is neither desirable nor, indeed, possible, for the notions of colloquial English to be rigidly tied to structural patterns. Nor has it been possible to exclude some of the more 'difficult' items of vocabulary from the earlier Units. As for the situations, they become gradually more complex towards the latter part of the book, leading the student into longer dialogues.

In the Introduction a general approach to the use of the book has already been suggested. The basis of the approach is role-playing: the students should think themselves into the roles of the characters in the dialogues. Some of the vocabulary and structure may already have been met by the student in reading texts but the important thing is to transfer this knowledge to active and instinctive use for a variety of practical purposes.

In Unit 17 we have revision of some of the main idiomatic phrases in previous Units, and in Units 17 and 18 there is some attention to more formal elements of discussion which some students may require for business purposes. We are assuming that your students may come from all walks of life and that as young or not-so-young adults they require added confidence in using colloquial English.

1 I'D LIKE TO BOOK A FLIGHT

Important words
- travel agency
- on business
- exhibition
- economy class
- change (v.)
- timetable
- airline
- voucher
- receipt
- air terminal
- check in
- reservation
- confirmation
- direct (adj.)
- insurance
- premium
- account
- valid
- claim (n.)

It was Monday morning and a lot of people were collecting tickets in the Gold Star travel agency. Among them were Mr and Mrs Taylor and their two children, Sarah and John. They were going on holiday to a small hotel on the coast of Arcania. Arcania is a small country in Asia. It was once under British rule, so many of the people there speak English.

Mr Robert Lee was also in the travel agency. He was going to Arcania as well, but he was going on business. He was going to arrange an exhibition for his company. Mr Lee's company publishes books and he sells books all over the world.

Mr Taylor had booked his family's air tickets earlier, but Mr Lee hadn't booked his tickets yet.

DIALOGUE A

Mr Lee: I'd like to book a flight to Palmville, please.
Clerk 1: Certainly, sir, single or return?
Mr Lee: Return, please, economy class. I believe there's a flight next Saturday.
Clerk 1: Just a minute, sir, I'll check . . . Sorry, sir, that's fully booked. But you can catch an SAS flight via Copenhagen – you change in Copenhagen.
Mr Lee: That sounds all right. Could I see the timetable?

DIALOGUE B

Mr Taylor: I believe our tickets are ready. My name's Taylor.
Clerk 2: That's right, sir, here's your folder – air tickets, airline labels, hotel voucher, everything's here. And here's your receipt.
Mr Taylor: Fine. What time must we be at the air terminal?
Clerk 2: Your flight leaves at 19.30 and you must check in at the terminal two hours before.

DIALOGUE C

Mr Lee: Could you make a hotel reservation for me?
Clerk 1: Yes, sir, which hotel?
Mr Lee: Hotel Samyra, if possible.
Clerk 1: Sorry?
Mr Lee: Samyra. S-A-M-Y-R-A.
Clerk 1: I see. OK, we'll get confirmation as soon as possible.

DIALOGUE D

Mrs Taylor: How long does the flight take? It's a direct flight, isn't it?
Clerk 2: Yes, the travelling time is nine and a half hours. You arrive in Palmville just after 11.00 am local time. Your connecting flight to Port Merlin leaves two hours later.
Mrs Taylor: I hope we don't miss it.

DIALOGUE E

Mr Lee: I'd like to pay by cheque. Is that all right?
Clerk 1: Yes, sir, if you have a banker's card.
Mr Lee: Oh yes, here you are.
Clerk 1: Right. Thank you, sir.

DIALOGUE F

Mr Taylor: Oh, one more thing. Is our travel insurance all right?
Clerk 2: Yes, sir. The premium was included in our account.
Mr Taylor: And it's valid for the full two weeks?
Clerk 2: Oh, yes. In fact you're covered for seventeen days. And there's a claims form in your folder.

Notes

economy class: Most airlines have at least two classes of travel, first class and economy class, which is cheaper.

a folder: A big, strong envelope.

a voucher: This is a piece of paper which says that you have paid for something. You can use it instead of money to pay for food, travel, etc.

the air terminal: An airline office in the city.

a banker's card: This card proves that the bank will support your cheque payment.

the premium: Money which you pay when you take out insurance.

a claims form: You fill in a claims form if you want to claim under your insurance.

COMPREHENSION QUESTIONS

(a) Why do people in Arcania speak English?
(b) Why was Mr Lee going to Arcania?
(c) What was Mr Lee going to do in Copenhagen?
(d) Had Mr Taylor paid for his family's holiday?
(e) When did the Taylor family have to check in at the air terminal?
(f) Where did the Taylors have to change?
(g) How long did the Taylors' travel insurance last?

4 I'D LIKE TO BOOK A FLIGHT

PRACTICE 1

Fill in the missing words.

Mr Lee was going to fly (1) .... Copenhagen to Arcania. He was going there to arrange a book (2) .... He asked the clerk for a hotel (3) .... in Palmville. When he paid for his ticket he showed his (4) ....

When the Taylors went to the (5) .... they collected a (6) .... full of travel papers. The clerk gave them the (7) .... for their payment. When Mr Taylor asked the clerk about their (8) .... he told them it was (9) .... for over two weeks. The (10) .... was included in the (11) .... that he had received.

PRACTICE 2

Practise this dialogue with the clerk (B).

A: I believe there's a (n) ....
B: That's right, sir. It leaves at 10.20.
A: OK, could you make a reservation for me?
B: Certainly, sir, single or return?

> SAS flight
> direct flight
> flight via Palmville
> connecting flight

PRACTICE 3

The clerk (B) is answering you. What did you say to him?

A: ....
B: Yes sir, they're in this folder.
A: ....
B: That's all right, sir. I'll give you a receipt.
A: ....
B: Two hours before the flight, sir.

I'D LIKE TO BOOK A FLIGHT 5

PRACTICE 4

Which sentences (including one-word sentences) in the dialogues mean:

(a) The flight takes nine and a half hours.
(b) That's a good plan.
(c) Very good!
(d) Could you please repeat that.
(e) Please take it.
(f) Your insurance lasts ....
(g) I understand.
(h) I nearly forgot to mention something.

FURTHER STUDY

Here is part of an airline timetable.

Day	Mon									Tue								Wed							
Flight No. Aircraft Class	KE 001 747 F/Y	KE 701 A300 F/Y	KE 703 A300 F/Y	KE 721 A300 F/Y	KE 723 707 F/Y	KE 733 707 Y	KE 731 707 Y	KE 751 707 F/Y	KE 767 707 F/Y	KE 701 A300 F/Y	KE 703 DC10 F/Y	KE 721 707 F/Y	KE 733 707 Y	KE 731 707 Y	KE 751 707 F/Y	KE 757 707 Y	KE 616 A300 F/Y	KE 001 747 F/Y	KE 703 DC10 F/Y	KE 721 707 F/Y	KE 723 707 F/Y	KE 733 707 Y	KE 731 707 Y	KE 751 707 F/Y	KE 767 A300 F/Y
Tokyo Dp	1720	1050	1330							1720	1330							1720	1330						
Nagoya Dp								1130																	1130
Osaka Dp				1100	1350			1800				1100			1800	1355	1550			1100	1350			1800	
Fukuoka Dp						1450	1140						1450	1140								1450	1140		
Pusan Ar Dp						1220	1915						1220	1915		1510 1550						1220	1915		
Cheju Ar																1630									
Seoul Ar	1930	1300	1540	1230	1520	1600			1310	1930	1540	1230	1600				1720	1930	1540	1230	1520	1600			1310

PRACTICE 5

Passenger (A) is in Osaka. Complete the following dialogue with the clerk (B).

A: .... Cheju, please.

B: Certainly, sir, single or return?
A: Return, please, economy class. .... next Monday.
B: Just a minute, I'll check . . . Sorry sir, there's no flight on Monday. But there's ....
A: That .... all right. How long ....?
B: ....

Here is a map with some information about travel.

Tourist Map of the Hallyo Coast

Transportation

By	From Seoul	Frequency	Duration	Fare
Express bus	Pusan	6.30–17.50 (10 min. intervals)	5 hrs 20 min.	US $15

Hydrofoil

From	To	Frequency	Duration	Fare
Pusan	Chungmu	6 times/day	1½ hrs	US $8.50
Chungmu	Yosu	3 times/day	1¾ hrs	US $9.20

Important words
express bus
hydrofoil
ferry
cabin
fare

How to get there

Express bus/Hydrofoil

A fast and comfortable express bus runs from Seoul to Pusan in less than 5½ hours. In Pusan you can change to the hydrofoil for Chungmu or Yosu. There are connections by air or by ferry (with cabins) between Pusan and Japan.

Notes

a hydrofoil: A hydrofoil stands up on the water. Compare this with a hovercraft, which flies on a layer of air.
a cabin: A private room on a ship.

PRACTICE 6

Two friends, (A) and (B), are talking in Seoul. Complete their conversation.

A: I'm going on .... next week.
B: Oh? Where to?
A: To Chungmu.
B: Where's that?
A: On the ....
B: How are you going there?
A: Well, I'm catching the .... bus to Pusan – they run every .... Then I'll catch the .... It's really very cheap – the .... from Pusan to Chungmu is less than .... And it only takes ....

Talking about insurance.

Here is part of an insurance certificate.

Section A
Medical and additional expenses. Age limit seventy-five. 50 per cent additional premium for ages over seventy but not exceeding seventy-five.
Maximum any one person £4000.
Special cancellation cover – air fare.

Section B
Personal accident. Age limit seventy-five.
Maximum any one person £25000.
Children aged under sixteen – maximum £5000.

Section C
Baggage and personal effects. Personal money.

| Group discount is allowed for parties of three or more insured under one certificate | Total sum insured £.......... Names of insured persons: .... |

Notes

cancellation cover: Insurance against cancelling something.
personal effects: Things that you own.
discount: A sum taken off the price.

Important words
certificate
medical
expenses
maximum
cancel(lation)
personal effects
baggage
discount

PRACTICE 7

(A) is talking to (B) about this company's insurance. Which of his statements are completely correct?

(a) You can't get travel insurance if you're over seventy.
(b) If you want medical insurance you can insure for any amount.
(c) If a husband and wife insure together they can get a discount.
(d) Anyone who has an accident can claim up to £25000.
(e) Some people can claim if they have to cancel their air ticket.

PRACTICE 8

Mr (A) is in Pusan and he is going to Japan on business. Last week he bought an air ticket. But now he has to take a lot of extra things for his company. So today he went to the travel agency. What did he say to the clerk (B)?

A: I bought this air ticket last week.
B: Yes, sir.
A: But now .... it because I want to travel by sea. I've got a lot of extra b.......... Could you .... on the .... ?
B: I'll try, sir.
A: How much is the single ....?
B: It's thirty-eight dollars, sir, or sixty if you want a ....
A: Well, that'll be more comfortable.

2 WHICH WAY DO I GO NOW?

Important words		
counter	platform	refreshment lounge
queue (n.)	in time	baggage tag
shoulder bag	passenger	passport control
luggage trolley	direction	announce
airport	weigh	sign board
briefcase	allowance	official (n.)
underground railway	overweight	arrow
rush-hour	non-smoking section	passage
booking-office	boarding card	

Mr and Mrs Taylor with Sarah and John checked in at the air terminal at 5.00 pm. They went to the check-in counter but had to wait about fifteen minutes as there was a long queue. They had a suitcase and a shoulder bag each and Mr Taylor carried a small luggage trolley.

Mr Lee planned to check in at the airport. He had a case and a briefcase. He decided to go to the airport by underground railway. As it was the beginning of the morning rush-hour the trains were crowded. He stopped at the booking-office, bought a ticket and then went to the wrong platform. But he arrived at the airport in time.

DIALOGUE A

Mr Lee: Excuse me, is this the right platform for the airport?
Passenger A: Well, no, you're going in the wrong direction.
Mr Lee: Oh, really?
Passenger A: Bill, where does the airport train go from?
Passenger B: Platform 2, I think.
Mr Lee: OK, thanks.

DIALOGUE B

Airline clerk 1: May I see your tickets and passports, please?
Mr Taylor: Here they are. Will you weigh all our baggage together?
Airline clerk 1: Yes, would you put it all on the machine, please.
Sarah: Dad, do I need to weigh my bag?
Mr Taylor: Yes, put everything together... Ah, seventy-eight kilos.
Mrs Taylor: Is that inside the free allowance?
Mr Taylor: Yes, we're allowed twenty kilos each.
Mrs Taylor: That's lucky!

DIALOGUE C

Airline clerk 2: I'm sorry, sir, you're five kilos overweight.
Mr Lee: I know, it's the books. Look, I'll take them out for reading on the plane. Is that all right?
Airline clerk 2: Well, yes, you can do that if you like.
Mr Lee: They weigh five and a half kilos. So then I'll be just under the weight.

DIALOGUE D

Airline clerk 1: Right, sir, you've got four seats in the non-smoking section. And here are your tickets for the airport bus.

12 WHICH WAY DO I GO NOW?

Mrs Taylor: Have you got the boarding cards?
Mr Taylor: Yes, dear, they're here. When does the next bus leave?
Airline clerk 1: At 5.30. They run every twenty minutes.
Mrs Taylor: I'd like some coffee. Where can we find the refreshment lounge?
Airline clerk 1: Just up the stairs, madam.

DIALOGUE E

Mr Lee: Have you booked my case through to Palmville?
Airline clerk 2: Yes sir. Your baggage tag is attached to your ticket.
Mr Lee: Which way do I go now?
Airline clerk 2: Passport control is that way. Then the departure lounge is straight ahead.

DIALOGUE F

John: Have I got time to buy a magazine?
Mr Taylor: I don't think so. They're announcing our flight.
John: Where?
Mr Taylor: On that sign board up there.
John: Oh yes. Gate 27. Which way is gate 27?
Mr Taylor: Here's someone in uniform. Excuse me, could you tell us the way to gate 27?
Airline official: Yes, do you see that arrow?
Mr Taylor: Yes.
Airline official: Start there and follow the passage. You'll soon find it, sir.

Notes

in time: Early enough (to catch his flight).
boarding cards: The boarding card proves that you have a seat on the plane. You show it when you board the plane.
booked . . . through: Mr Lee is changing planes in Copenhagen but he'll collect his case in Palmville. He'll get it back when he shows his baggage tag.
passport control: The place where passports are checked.
gate: The exit which leads to the plane is called a 'gate'.

COMPREHENSION QUESTIONS

(a) How many pieces of luggage did the Taylors have altogether?
(b) Why were the trains crowded?
(c) Why was Mrs Taylor happy about the luggage?
(d) How much did Mr Lee's suitcase weigh when he took it to the counter?
(e) Do you think Mr Taylor is a smoker?

PRACTICE 1

Fill in the missing words.

Mr Lee arrived at the airport by (1) .... and went straight to the airline (2) c......... where he nearly had to pay extra because his case and (3) .... were five kilos (4) .... The Taylors, however, were lucky because they were just inside the (5) .... When they arrived in the (6) .... the airline was already (7) .... their flight on the (8) .... They had to follow a long (9) .... to find the (10) .... for their flight.

PRACTICE 2

Practise this dialogue with the airline clerk (B).

A: Excuse me, is this the right ....?
B: No, you've come to the wrong floor. Go to the end of that passage and take the lift to the ground floor.
A: Oh, thanks very much.

> counter for Arcanian Airways
> queue for the airport bus
> gate for flight 123

PRACTICE 3

What do you ask the clerk at the airline counter?

(a) You're looking for the departure lounge.
(b) You don't know which way to go next.
(c) You aren't sure about weighing your briefcase.

14 WHICH WAY DO I GO NOW?

(d) You want to know if you can have some coffee before your flight.
(e) You want to know if he has put labels for London on your suitcase.

PRACTICE 4

How can you make these requests more polite?

(a) Put all your luggage on the machine.
(b) Show me your baggage tag.
(c) Give me a seat in the non-smoking section.
(d) Book my case through to Port Merlin.

FURTHER STUDY

Here is part of an airline notice about baggage.

> **Important words**
> dimensions
> pushchair
> hand baggage

Baggage

Each passenger of more than two years of age has a free baggage allowance.

Generally this limit is 20 kg (44 lb) for economy-class passengers and 30 kg (66 lb) for first-class passengers. However, for travel to/from USA and US territories the free baggage allowance is limited as follows:

(a) Checked baggage
(1) First-class passengers:
   Two pieces of baggage of which the sum of the three dimensions (length, width, height) of each bag does not exceed 62 inches (158 cm), provided that each bag does not weigh more than 35 kg.
(2) Economy-class passengers:
   Two pieces of baggage of which the sum of the total dimensions

does not exceed 106 inches (270 cm), provided that neither bag exceeds 62 inches (158 cm) or does not weigh more than 35 kg.

(b) Unchecked baggage
First/economy-class passengers:
One piece of hand baggage of which the sum of the total dimensions does not exceed 45 inches (115 cm).

(c) Infants
Infants paying 10 per cent of the fare are allowed one piece of checked baggage of which the sum of the three dimensions does not exceed 39 inches (100 cm) plus one checked fully collapsible pushchair.

The following articles will be carried free of charge in the cabin and will not be weighed: a lady's handbag, an umbrella or walking-stick, an overcoat or wrap, a small camera and a pair of binoculars, a reasonable quantity of reading material, an infant's carrying basket and baby food, a fully collapsible wheelchair or a pair of crutches.

Excess baggage charges

Baggage in excess of the free baggage allowance will result in excess baggage charges.

Notes

provided that: A stronger form of 'if'.
an infant: A child up to about two years old.
collapsible: Which can fold up.
the cabin: A special use of this word. It means the passenger area of a plane.
a wrap: A cover which you can wrap around yourself.
reasonable: Not too large.
in excess of: More than.

PRACTICE 5

Passenger (A) was talking to the airline clerk (B) about weighing his wife's handbag. What did he say?

A: .... her handbag?
B: No sir, that's carried free of charge.
A: That's ....! It's heavier than my briefcase.

PRACTICE 6

What do these phrases/sentences mean in conversational English?

(a) More than two years of age.
(b) The dimensions of the case (length, width, height) are 28, 5 and 18 inches.
(c) Baggage in excess of the free baggage allowance will result in excess baggage charges.

PRACTICE 7

What did the airline clerk answer when you telephoned him with this question?

I'm an economy-class passenger flying to the USA. I've got two cases, one weighs 30 kilos and the other 28 kilos and each of them measures 28 by 17 by 8 inches. Must I pay excess?

Some information for travellers to Heathrow Airport, London

Underground to Heathrow

Because the new Heathrow Central station connects the Piccadilly Line to all three Heathrow terminals you can get from the nearest London Underground station to your departure lounge – under cover all the way.

The Piccadilly Line has been specially replanned to meet the increased demand. Open 20 hours a day (18 hours on Sundays) on every day of the week, it runs at least 8 trains an hour and, at weekday morning and evening peaks, 15 trains an hour – that's a train every four minutes. No more traffic jams and parking problems.

And when you're on your way back to central London from Heathrow you can reach your destination easily by Underground. There are guidebooks and maps which will give you detailed information about your route.

Have a good trip!

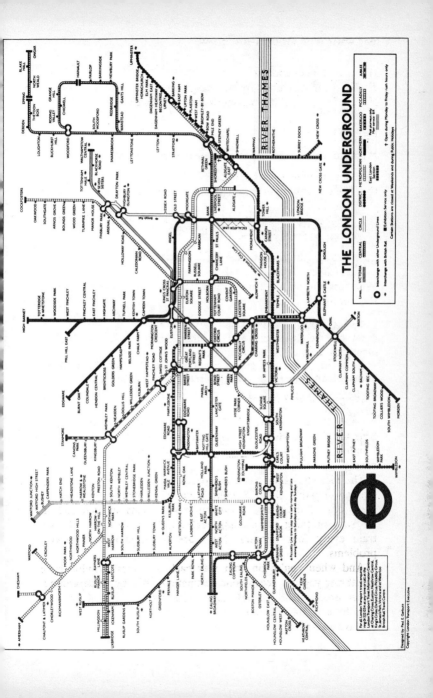

Important words
traffic jam
park(ing)
destination
trip
route

Notes

the increased demand: The extra passengers.
peaks: Rush-hour times.
Heathrow terminals: At some big airports the place where you
 check in is called a terminal.

PRACTICE 8

'Excuse me, how do I get to Heathrow Central from here?' What answer do you expect at the following London Underground stations (to help you find them the line is given)? The first answer is also given as an example.

(a) Queen's Park (Bakerloo Line)
    (Change at Paddington, take the Metropolitan Line to
    Hammersmith and then the Piccadilly Line.)
(b) Queensway (Central Line)
(c) Regents Park (Bakerloo Line)
(d) West Hampstead (Jubilee Line)
(e) Clapham North (Northern Line)
(f) Mornington Crescent (Northern Line)

PRACTICE 9

Finish the statements under these cartoons. Choose words from the box below.

Flying into Heathrow – flying out of Heathrow.

Look for the .... and follow it to the trains. You can't go wrong!

Children .... travel at less than half ....

Press the button for your .... The complete .... will appear on the screen.

The Piccadilly Line .... Heathrow with most areas of .... London.

You can get all the way to Heathrow ....

Carriages are specially built with .... space for ....

Relax. We'll get you to the plane .... Have a good ....

All the .... operating from all three .... are indicated as you leave the ....

airlines	terminals	extra
under 12 years of age	platform	central
connects	fare	destination
luggage	Underground sign	under cover
route plan	trip	in time

PRACTICE 10

Which statements above answer these questions?

(a) How do I get to this station, please?
(b) Could you tell me the way to the Underground?

3 THEY'RE ASKING US TO FASTEN OUR SEAT BELTS

Important words		
fasten	transit	take-off (n.)
seat belt	security check	refund (n.)
life jacket	board (v.)	steward(ess)
take off (v.)	on board	land (v.)
delay (n.)	row (n.)	temperature
air hostess	duty free	immigration
soft drink	carton	arrival
earphones	pilot	fill in
landing card	crew	Customs
on time	aircraft	

Mr and Mrs Taylor's plane took off after a delay of forty minutes. Sarah, who is often travel sick, kept a paper bag ready. John read the airline magazine and followed their route on the map. When the air hostess came round with the trolley Mrs Taylor ordered a soft drink and Mr Taylor bought a beer. After dinner they got earphones, listened to some music and watched a film. Before arriving in Palmville they had to fill in landing cards.

Mr Lee's flight to Copenhagen left on time. After landing he went with the other transit passengers to the transit lounge. After going through another security check he boarded the Palmville flight. When he got on board he changed seats with an American passenger who wanted a seat in the same row as his family. After the bar opened Mr Lee bought a bottle of duty-free whisky and a carton of cigarettes.

DIALOGUE A

Pilot: On behalf of British Airways Captain Allen and his crew would like to welcome you on board this aircraft. We apologise for the delay but we'll be taking off shortly.
Mr Taylor: Excuse me, when will you serve drinks?
Air hostess: I'll be bringing the trolley round soon after take-off sir.
Mr Taylor: Good. Thanks.
Mrs Taylor: Could I have a blanket for my daughter, please?
Air hostess: I'll get you one, madam.

DIALOGUE B

Passenger A: Excuse me, is this seat free?
Mr Lee: Sorry, it's taken. I'm just going to sit down.
Passenger A: Well . . . would you mind changing places with me? Then I can sit next to my family.
Mr Lee: Oh, I see. No, I don't mind.
Passenger A: Thanks very much.
Mr Lee: Not at all.

DIALOGUE C

John: Dad, there's something wrong with my earphones. I can't hear anything.
Mr Taylor: Really? Try mine.
John: These don't work either.
Mr Taylor: OK, I'll tell the stewardess. Er, sorry, but my son can't get any sound. And he's paid for the earphones.

Air hostess: Sorry about that, sir. Perhaps it's the seat. I'll have to give you a refund.

DIALOGUE D

Passenger B: Oh, steward.
Steward: Yes, sir?
Passenger B: Isn't this a non-smoking area?
Steward: That's right.
Passenger B: Well, would you ask that passenger not to smoke?
Steward: Er . . . yes, all right. Excuse me, sir, this area is for non-smokers. Do you mind not smoking?
Mr Lee: What? Oh yes, sorry.

DIALOGUE E

Mrs Taylor: What was that announcement, Jim?
Mr Taylor: They're asking us to fasten our seat belts.
Mrs Taylor: Why? What's happened?
Mr Taylor: Don't worry, everything's fine. We're probably going through some bad weather.

DIALOGUE F

Pilot: Ladies and gentlemen, we shall shortly be landing at Halo airport, Palmville. Local time is five thirty in the afternoon and local weather conditions are slightly cloudy. The outside temperature is twenty-eight degrees.
Passenger C: Well, we're arriving on time. Er . . . what do we do with our landing cards?
Mr Lee: They're for the immigration officer on arrival.
Passenger C: I haven't filled mine in yet. Would you mind lending me your pen?
Mr Lee: Sure, here you are.

Notes

an air hostess: Air hostesses (stewardesses) and stewards are also often called flight attendants.

24 THEY'RE ASKING US TO FASTEN OUR SEAT BELTS

a soft drink: A fruit drink which contains no alcohol.
on time: At the correct time.
transit: If you are in transit you haven't finished your journey.
a security check: A check for weapons.
duty free: Free of Customs duty (Customs tax).
we'll be taking off: This tense, the future continuous, is often used during travel for official announcements.
a refund: If you get a refund you get your money back.
immigration: Entry into a country.

COMPREHENSION QUESTIONS

(a) What was the actual departure time of the Taylors' flight?
(b) Why did Mr Lee change seats?
(c) Why was Mrs Taylor worried?
(d) Was Mr Lee's flight to Copenhagen delayed?
(e) Did Mr Lee's flight arrive late in Palmville?
(f) What did the passenger borrow from Mr Lee?

PRACTICE 1

Fill in the missing words.

A: Sorry, but I'm feeling a bit sick.
B: But we haven't even (1) .... yet!
A: I know, but this always happens when they tell us to (2) .... our (3) ....
B: Would you like to sit in my seat, away from the window? I'll (4) .... places if you like.
A: No, I'll stay here, thanks. I'll probably be all right after (5) .... How much longer will the (6) .... be?
B: A few more minutes, I think. Here comes the (7) .... I'll ask him.
A: Would you mind passing that bag over?
B: (8) ...., here you are.

PRACTICE 2

Practise this dialogue with passenger (A).

A: What was that announcement?

B: They .... us ....
A: I see, thanks.

're asking 're telling told	to fill in our landing cards to go through the security check not to smoke not to forget our hand baggage

PRACTICE 3

The future continuous tense is often used during travel. What answers can the passengers expect when they ask the stewardess these questions (supply your own adverb phrases)?

(a) When do we take off, please?
(b) Is the bar open, please?
(c) When will you give out landing cards, please?
(d) What time do we arrive at Palmville, please?

PRACTICE 4

Can you fill in the missing parts of these dialogues?

(a) *A*: .... the luggage trolley.
    B: Oh? What's happened to it?
    A: The wheels won't turn.
(b) *A*: ....?
    B: No, I don't mind. Anyway, I'm not listening to the music.
    A: Thanks very much.
    B: ....
(c) *A*: Excuse me, steward, ...?
    B: Thirty-two C. That's right sir.
    A: Well, why is someone sitting in it?
(d) *A*: ...., please?
    B: Yes madam, what would you like. Orange juice? Coca cola?

FURTHER STUDY

Here is some useful information for air travellers from an airline notice.

> **Important words**
> storage compartment switch on article
> medicine portable belongings
> available tape recorder (dis)embark
> prohibited

Welcome aboard

Your captain and crew are very happy to have you on board and will do everything possible to make your journey pleasant and memorable.

Please do not hesitate to use the call button for service.

Our cabin crew will be happy to assist you.

Pillows and blankets: These are stored in the overhead storage compartments.

In flight entertainment: Our aircraft are equipped with in flight music channels. The cabin crew will supply you with earphones.

Writing material: Airline postcards and air letters should be handed to the cabin crew who will post them free of charge.

Children and infants: For children we have drawing books and games; for infants a small variety of baby foods is available from your stewardess.

Medicines: For treatment of minor discomforts medicines are available from your cabin crew.

Games: For your entertainment we carry chess sets, draughts, playing cards and reading material.

Toiletry items: Toothbrushes, towels, soap, etc., are available. Men's and women's toiletries such as cologne, aftershave lotion and skin tonic are also available. Shaving equipment is available on request from the cabin crew.

Smoking: Smoking is not permitted while the aircraft is on the ground or during take-off and landing and is strictly prohibited in the aircraft toilets. Smoking is confined to cigarettes only. Passengers are requested to refrain from smoking in the non-smoking sections of the cabin. Pipe smoking is not allowed in any aircraft.

Fasten seat belt: We suggest that you keep your seat belt loosely fastened at all times while you are seated.

Portable radio and TV sets: The operation of portable radio and TV sets can interfere with the aircraft's radio navigation equipment and therefore should not be switched on during flight. Portable tape recorders and hearing aids are permissible.

Your personal belongings: Please do not leave small articles of value on board the aircraft at transit stops and be sure to check that you have all your belongings when you disembark.

Duty-free goods: The amount of duty-free goods allowed into each country varies considerably. Your cabin crew will advise you of the limits.

Notes

draughts: You may know this game by its American name – checkers.
cologne: A kind of perfume.
is confined to: Is limited to.
to refrain from smoking: Not to smoke.
navigation: Finding the way by instruments, etc.
portable: Small, suitable for carrying.
embark/disembark: To go on board/to leave an aircraft or ship.
varies considerably: Is very different.

PRACTICE 5

You are flying by Arcanian Airways. Answer these questions about your flight.

(a) Where can you store your briefcase, handbag, etc.?
(b) Where and when is smoking not allowed?
(c) What kinds of entertainment are available?
(d) What kinds of entertainment are not allowed?
(e) What information can the cabin crew give you?
(f) You needn't bring soap and towels with you. Why not?
(g) Do you need to bring games for your children?

PRACTICE 6

Fill in the missing words.

Would (1) .... passengers please go to the (2) .... lounge. Please take all your valuable (3) .... with you when you (4) .... Before you (5) .... the (6) .... again you will have to go through another (7) .... check. Please note that smoking is (8) .... until you reach the terminal building.

PRACTICE 7

You are a flight attendant. What do you say to a passenger in these situations?

(a) A lady is smoking before take-off.
(b) A man is smoking a pipe.
(c) A lady has switched on her portable radio.
(d) A transit passenger has left her camera on the seat.

PRACTICE 8

Two passengers who met on flight AX 123 from Copenhagen to Palmville are talking about their plans there. How much of their landing cards can you fill in from their conversation?

A.
- Please type or print with a ball-point pen
- Do not write in box ☐ • Do not fold
- Give CARD 2 to the immigration officer at the time of your departure from or re-entry into Arcania.

XY 401212

.... ☐1 ☐2
                                                    Male   Female

Family name ....
Given names ....
Date of birth.................. Day/ .... Month/19..... Year
Nationality .... Passport no ....
Occupation ....
Home address ....
Address in Arcania ....
Purpose of visit ....

```
Intended length of stay in Arcania ................................................
Flight no./Vessel ................................................
Port of embarkation ................................................
Port of disembarkation ................................................
Signature ................................................
```

For official use only [ ]

B.
- Please type or print with a ball-point pen
- Do not write in box ☐   • Do not fold
- Give CARD 2 to the immigration officer at the time of your departure from or re-entry into Arcania.

XY 401213

.... [1] Male   [2] Female

```
Family name ................................................
Given names ................................................
Date of birth.................. Day/ .................. Month/19..... Year
Nationality ................................................ Passport no. ............
Occupation ................................................
Home address ................................................
Address in Arcania ................................................
Purpose of visit ................................................
Intended length of stay in Arcania ................................................
Flight no./Vessel ................................................
Port of embarkation ................................................
Port of disembarkation ................................................
Signature ................................................
```

For official use only [ ]

A: Where are you from?
B: I'm from Sydney, Australia. How about you?
A: I'm from New York.
B: Are you staying in Arcania long?
A: Only a couple of weeks.
B: I'm here for two months.
A: That's quite a long time.

B: Yes, I'm opening a new office for my company.
A: Where are you staying?
B: At the Scala Hotel. And you?
A: Oh, I'll be staying with friends at the Embassy. Here's the address. My name's Green. Harry Green.
B: I'm John Merton. Pleased to meet you.

Here is some information from a guidebook to Palmville.

Important words
guidebook
harbour
quay
public holiday
service
deck
invalid (n.)
barrier
turnstile
gangway
taxi rank
hire

The most popular cross-harbour passenger ferry is the Alice Ferry which runs from Biltong Quay (almost opposite the Scala Hotel) to Lama Bay, taking thirty minutes. The ferries run every forty minutes during the day on weekdays and every thirty minutes on Sundays and public holidays, starting at five thirty in the morning until late at night. All-night services are run on Christmas Eve and New Year's Eve.

The one-way fare is twenty dinars first class and twelve dinars second class (this is downstairs and rather hot as the engine room occupies part of the lower deck). Travelling first class you have to climb some stairs but not by second class – this is important for invalids. For the same reason it is easier to take luggage by second class. You deposit your luggage at the barrier (which is guarded by officials), pass through the turnstile and then return to collect your belongings which you then carry along the gangway. Alternatively you can hire a porter and take him all the way with you on the ferry to Lama Bay. You will find his services especially necessary here as the taxi rank is a long way from the ferry exit. In wet weather you will be soaked and there will probably be a long queue. If you prefer to deposit your bags and look for a taxi elsewhere, there is a left luggage office.

Notes

the deck: The floor of a ship (sometimes also used of aircraft).
a gangway: A moveable walk-way, leading to a ship.
a taxi rank: The place where you catch taxis.

PRACTICE 9

What do you know about the Alice Ferry? Fill in the missing words in these dialogues.

(a) *Passenger*: Have we missed the last ferry?
    Official: No, you needn't worry. There's an .... today.
    Passenger: Really?
    Official: Yes, it's .... today.
    Passenger: Ah, of course. That's lucky.
(b) *Passenger A*: What did that porter say?
    Passenger B: He's telling us to travel ....
    Passenger A: Why?
    Passenger B: Well, because of your bad leg. He says .... usually travel ....
    Passenger A: Nonsense. It's much too hot down there. We'll be sitting next to ....
    Passenger B: But can you ....?
    Passenger A: Of course I can.
(c) *Official*: Here is an announcement. Would passengers please .... their luggage at ...., go .... and then return to .... Please show your ticket again before you pass along ....
    Passenger: I'm going to .... Then he can come .... to the .... at ....

4 I HOPE WE HAVEN'T MISSED OUR CONNECTION

Important words

connection
foreigner
domestic flight
missing
visa

businessman
tourist
exchange bureau
traveller's cheque
currency

public transport
initial (n.)
rate of exchange
slip (n.)

When the Taylors arrived in Palmville they went down the steps and boarded a bus which took them to the terminal building. It was a very busy time – hundreds of passengers were arriving on different flights. Before immigration there was a health check – all passengers had to show their health certificates. From there they went to Immigration where they showed their passports and handed in their landing cards. Then they collected their suitcases and went through Customs. There was a long queue at every Customs counter. Some counters were for foreigners, some for Arcanians. The queues for foreigners were moving fairly quickly – the Customs officers weren't opening every bag. The Taylors had to go quickly to the check-in counter for their domestic flight to Port Merlin and they had just enough time to catch it. But when they arrived at Port Merlin they had a problem – one of their suitcases was missing.

Mr Lee's flight arrived early in the evening. The immigration officer looked at his visa (businessmen travelling to Arcania need visas although tourists don't) and the Customs officer asked him to open his case. The exchange bureau was still open so he changed some traveller's cheques into Arcanian currency. In the entrance hall he was met by Mr Kay, his company's agent, and they went by car to the hotel. There is public transport from the airport at Palmville but it is rather slow and there is no airport bus.

DIALOGUE A

Customs officer: Is this all your luggage?
Mr Lee: Yes, it's all here.
Customs officer: Would you open this one, please.
Mr Lee: Right . . . Sorry, it's a bit difficult to open. There's something wrong with the lock . . . there.

DIALOGUE B

Mrs Taylor: I hope we haven't missed our connection.
Mr Taylor: We should be all right. It's just twelve o'clock. Let's find the domestic flight counter.
Mrs Taylor: Look – the exchange bureau. Don't forget to change some money.
Mr Taylor: There isn't time for that now. We'll get some in Port Merlin.

DIALOGUE C

Customs officer: How long are you staying in Arcania?
Mr Lee: Ten days. I'm here on business.
Customs officer: Is this a new tape recorder?
Mr Lee: No, it's two years old. I have a receipt for it.
Customs officer: All right. Have a pleasant stay.
Mr Lee: Thank you.

DIALOGUE D

Airline official: Can I help you?
Mr Taylor: Yes, we have a problem. One of our suitcases is missing. It was booked on to this flight. Could you help us to find it?
Mrs Taylor: It's full of clothes. We must have it.
Airline official: I see. Well, would you give me your tickets and baggage tags, sir. I'll check with the aircraft. Can you describe the suitcase?
Mr Taylor: Yes, it's light blue with soft sides and it's got my initials on it, J.R.T.
Airline official: OK, please wait here and I'll see what I can do.

DIALOGUE E

Mr Lee: I'd like to change seventy pounds, please. What's the rate of exchange today?
Clerk: It's four point seven five dinars to the pound. May I see your passport please?
Mr Lee: Here you are.
Clerk: You haven't signed one of these cheques.
Mr Lee: Ah, sorry. I'll do it now.
Clerk: Now, if you show this pink slip when you leave the country you can change dinars back into pounds.
Mr Lee: I'll remember that, thanks.

DIALOGUE F

Airline official: I've got some good news for you. They've got your suitcase in Palmville.
Mr Taylor: Thanks very much. So when can we get it?
Mrs Taylor: Yes, we need it soon.
Airline official: Well, there's another flight arriving at seven this evening. If you let me know the name of your hotel we'll deliver the case.
Mr Taylor: That's very kind of you, thanks.

Notes

a domestic flight: A flight by a country's internal airlines.

a visa: A visa (a stamp in your passport) is needed for entry into certain countries.

an agent: A local person who works for an overseas company.

COMPREHENSION QUESTIONS

(a) When passengers arrive at Halo airport, what three places do they go through?
(b) How do you get from Halo airport to Palmville?
(c) Why didn't the Taylors change money in Palmville?
(d) What is Arcanian currency called?
(e) How will the Taylors get their case?

PRACTICE 1

Fill in the missing words.

There wasn't time to get a (1) .... for Arcania before I left but luckily they gave me one on (2) .... in Palmville. I had to pay the (3) .... ten dinars and as I had no Arcanian (4) .... I had to change some (5) .... at the (6) .... (the (7) .... was just under five dinars (8) .... the pound).

PRACTICE 2

Practise this dialogue with the airline official.

Passenger: I hope ....
Airline official: Don't worry, I'll see what I can do.

> we don't miss our connection
> they haven't lost our suitcase
> there's time to change some money
> there's nothing wrong with the reservation

PRACTICE 3

Mr Taylor had a conversation with the Customs officer about his camera, which he bought just over a year ago (but he has lost the receipt). What did he say? (Dialogue C will help you.)

PRACTICE 4

John Merton, who was on the Copenhagen to Palmville flight, can't find his black leather briefcase. It has some important papers in it and his initials are on it. He told an airline official about it. What did they say? (Dialogue D will help you.)

FURTHER STUDY

Here is some important information about immigration for travellers to Arcania.

Important words
frontier
employment
applicant
ashore
issue (v.)
application
apply (for)
dependant (n.)
call (at)

Frontier formalities

All visitors to Arcania require:
- a valid vaccination certificate against smallpox,
- a valid vaccination certificate against yellow fever if coming from an infected area,
- sufficient funds in foreign exchange for maintenance in Arcania,
- an onward or return ticket.

Visas

Nationals of the following countries coming to Arcania as bona-fide tourists, that is for any legitimate non-immigrant purpose such as touring, recreation, sport, health, family reasons, study or religious pilgrimage, do not require visas.

Britain and colonies, Canada, Eire, Malaysia, Pakistan, Singapore	Six months' stay without visa
Australia, Austria, Belgium, Denmark, Federal Republic of Germany, Finland, France, Indonesia, Italy, Japan, Luxembourg, Netherlands, New Zealand, Sweden, Switzerland, USA	One month's stay without visa

Nationals of the above countries require a visa for entry into Arcania if they are not coming as bona-fide tourists but for other purposes such as business or employment.

Visit visas – are issued for a stay up to a maximum of six months and are normally valid for a single entry into Arcania. A double entry visa is granted without additional fee if the applicant so requests.

Transit visas – are issued to passengers desiring to disembark in Arcania in order to continue their journey by a different ship or aircraft. Transit visas are not required by passengers coming ashore during a ship's stay in port or by those continuing their journey in the same aircraft. A transit visa may be issued for a period not exceeding one month.

Residence visas – are issued for a stay exceeding six months for employment. These visas are issued only by the Controller of Immigration and Emigration, Government House, Palmville.

Application for a visa

The application should be made at least two weeks before the planned travel date.

The application form for the visa should be obtained from the issuing authority (usually the consular section of an Arcanian embassy).

Two photographs of passport size, together with the passport, should be submitted along with the application.

A parent or guardian may apply for a visa on behalf of a child or dependant under sixteen years of age.

Notes

formalities: Things that you must do.
funds: Money.
foreign exchange: Foreign money.
an infected area: An area where these diseases occur.
maintenance: The cost of supporting oneself.
nationals: Citizens.
immigrant: In this sense, someone coming to live in a country for a long time.
bona-fide: Real, true.
recreation: Any activity done for pleasure.
ashore: On (to) the land.
residence: Staying for a long time; living at a place.
an authority: An office with special powers.
a guardian: In this sense, someone who looks after a child who is not their own child.
a dependant: Someone who depends on you for support.

PRACTICE 5

Complete the following conversations (which took place at the Arcanian Embassy in London) with (B), the Consular clerk.

(a) *A*: I'm a Canadian citizen and I hope to go to Arcania on holiday. Do I need a visa, please?
   B: ....?
   A: Six weeks.
   B: Then you don't need a visa, not if you're a tourist.

(b) *A*: I'm hoping to go to Arcania for about two months. .... a visa?
   B: Which .... from?
   A: New Zealand.
   B: Yes, you'll have to .... a .... visa.
   A: OK, how do I ....?
   B: Here's .... please .... it .... and send it back with .... and ....
   A: I'd like to travel on 15 June.
   B: Then you should return your .... by .... at the latest.

(c) *A*: I'm making a journey by sea and the ship will be .... at Palmville for a few hours. I'd like to go ...., so I'd like to get a visa.

B: .... if you're only going .... for a few hours.

(d) *A*: Excuse me, I'm a teacher and I hope to get a job in Arcania for about a year. Can you give me a visa?

B: I'm sorry, we don't .... for .... You'll have to .... the Controller for Immigration in Palmville.

(e) *A*: I'm applying for a visit visa and I want to make two journeys to your country while the visa is valid. Do I have to pay any extra?

B: ....

PRACTICE 6

Fill in the missing words.

The Arcanian Embassy received twenty-five (1) .... for visas that week. They (2) .... twenty visas but the other five (3) .... had to wait. In one case the photographs were (4) .... from the form. In another case the passport was no longer (5) .... One woman (6) .... eight visas for herself and seven (7) .... The clerk asked her to (8) .... at the Embassy to discuss the matter.

And here is some information about Customs.

Customs hints for visitors

> **Important words**
> declaration   accompany   declare   import (v.)

1 Accompanied baggage

An oral declaration normally suffices for accompanied baggage. However, a written declaration is required in the case of the following articles: jewellery, articles made of precious metals, valuable watches and cameras, various valuable furs, firearms, knives and swords.

Failure to make a Customs declaration is punishable by law. Customs declaration forms are available on vessels, aircraft and at the Customs office.

2 Unaccompanied baggage

When baggage arrives separately a written import declaration form must be submitted within six months of your arrival if the baggage is to be recognised as personal baggage or household effects. If there are duty-free articles in the baggage shipped, a list itemising the articles must be attached to the declaration form.

Notes

suffices for: Is enough for.
an oral declaration: You declare (say) that you have certain articles.
failure to make: If you don't make.
is punishable: May be punished.
must be submitted: Must be made.
household effects: Things that are used in a house.
itemising: Giving in a certain order.

PRACTICE 7

Complete the following conversations between passengers and a Customs Officer (A).

(a) *A*: Is this all your luggage?
    B: Yes.
    A: Have you anything to ....?
    B: I've got this watch.
    A: May I see it, please. When did you buy it?
    B: It's new. I bought it yesterday.
    A: This is a .... watch, so you'll have to pay .... on it.
(b) *A*: Do you have any ....?
    B: Yes, it'll .... by sea in about a week's time.
    A: Have you .... a .... form?
    B: No, not yet.
    A: Well, take one of these.
    B: Can I get the baggage quickly after it arrives – all my household effects are in it?

A: I'll see ....
B: That's ...., thanks.

PRACTICE 8

A passenger (A) is leaving Arcania and he wants to change some Arcanian currency back into US dollars. What did he say to the clerk (B)?

A: I'd like to .... What's the .... today?
B: US dollars? It's two point six nought ....
A: Here's the .... that I got when I arrived.
B: May I know your name, please?
A: Boswell. It's written at the bottom.
B: Sorry, it's .... to read.

PRACTICE 9

> **Important words**
> conductor
> put off
> get off

Two students, Harry and Hilda, arrived on the same flight as Mr Lee. They wanted to go into Palmville by public transport. They wanted to know the number of the bus and where to catch it, the number of stops and the cost of a ticket. They wanted the conductor to put them off as near as possible to the tourist information office. Can you complete their conversation with the people who helped them?

Harry: Excuse me, which bus .... city centre?
Policeman: You want a number 5 or a number 13.
Harry: Ah, thanks, and ....?
Policeman: The bus-stop's over there under those trees.
Hilda: Come on, there's a number 13 now.

Harry: How much is it to the city centre, please?
Conductor: .... get off?
Harry: ....

Conductor: That's five dinars fifty cents each. Get off at Victory Gate.
Hilda: Could you please .... when we get there?
Conductor: OK, I'll tell you.
Hilda: Look, there's a map on the wall. It's twelve .... to Victory Gate.

5 CAN YOU FIND OUT HOW TO TURN THE WATER ON?

Important words

manage
cottage
arrangements
sort out
complain
management
reception

according to
out of date
roof rack
air-conditioned
double bed
twin beds

flush (v.)
socket
night club
(do one's) best
dial (v.)
maid

The Taylors decided to take a taxi to their hotel. A porter led them through the terminal building and they came to a taxi rank just outside the exit. They saw a notice with a list of taxi fares to various local hotels. Several taxi drivers were standing near it. They asked one of the drivers to take them but they had an argument about the fare. The driver's price was higher than the sum that the notice mentioned but in the end they agreed on a price. It was a small taxi, so it was hard to get all the luggage and passengers in but eventually they **managed it. Their hotel stood in a grove of palm** trees on the edge **of a beautiful bay about half an hour's drive from** the airport. After **they had checked in the manager's wife took t**hem to one of the hotel **cottages. At first they had some difficulties w**ith the sleeping arrangements and a problem with the water but eventually they managed to sort everything out by moving to another cottage.

Mr Lee also had some trouble. He complained to the hotel management because his room was too noisy. He rang the reception desk and succeeded in changing rooms.

DIALOGUE A

Mr Taylor: Let's find out where to get a taxi. Porter, the taxi rank, please.
Mrs Taylor: How far do we have to go?
Mr Taylor: A few yards, I expect. There's probably one near here.
Mrs Taylor: No, I mean to the hotel.
Mr Taylor: Oh, I think it's about twenty kilometres.
John: Dad, here are the taxis.
Mr Taylor: Right, let's pay the porter – seven pieces of luggage, what's that?
John: Three dinars fifty cents – I worked it out!
Mrs Taylor: Ought we to tip him?
Mr Taylor: I don't think we need to. He hasn't brought them far.

DIALOGUE B

Mr Taylor: Could you take us to Diamond Beach Inn, please?
Taxi driver: OK, that'll be forty dinars.
Mr Taylor: Forty? But according to that notice it's twenty-five.
Taxi driver: That notice is out of date, sir. (to his friends) That's right, isn't it?
Other drivers: Sure, that's right.
Mr Taylor: But look, it's dated 1 July – that's only a month ago. All right, thirty dinars.
Taxi driver: Thirty-five.
Mr Taylor: Well, . . . OK, but you're asking too much.

DIALOGUE C

Mr Taylor: Be careful of that suitcase. It's too big to go on top there.
Mrs Taylor: Yes, mind the lid.
Mr Taylor: Why can't we take it inside? It'll go on my lap.
Taxi driver: No problem. I'll borrow my friend's roof rack. Just a minute.

DIALOGUE D

Mr Lee: My name's Lee. I believe you have a reservation for me.
Hotel clerk: Mr Robert Lee from London?
Mr Lee: Right.
Hotel clerk: Yes sir. Number 817. Air-conditioned with private bathroom. I'll get the porter to take your bags up.
Mr Kay: I'll wait down here.
Mr Lee: Yes, I'll just sort things out, then let's have a drink.

DIALOGUE E

Sarah: Mum!
Mrs Taylor: What's the matter?
Sarah: We've got a double bed in here. Can't we have twin beds?
Mr Taylor: Don't worry. I'll get them to change it.
Mrs Taylor: Jim, I can't flush the toilet. Can you find out how to turn the water on?
Mr Taylor: All right, just coming. I'm trying to find a socket for my shaver.
John: Hey, there's no bath and I don't like having showers.
Mrs Taylor: Oh, you'll soon get used to it.

DIALOGUE F

Mr Lee (on the telephone): Hello, reception?
Hotel clerk: Yes sir?
Mr Lee: Could you possibly change my room – it's right under the night club and it's much too noisy.
Hotel clerk: Well, we are rather full, sir.
Mr Lee: Could you please try?
Hotel clerk: Very well, sir. I'll do my best.

Notes

a cottage: A very small house (in this case, part of the hotel accommodation).

an inn: A smaller type of hotel.

air-conditioned: Having an air-conditioner (a machine for cooling).

twin beds: Two single beds.

flush: This verb is both transitive and intransitive.

a socket: A place on the wall for electrical connections.

a night club: A club for late-night dancing.

COMPREHENSION QUESTIONS

(a) How did the Taylors know the correct taxi fare?
(b) What price did Mr Taylor and the taxi driver agree on?
(c) What kind of accommodation did the Taylors have at their hotel?
(d) What happened when the driver couldn't get all the luggage in – what did he do?
(e) What complaints did the Taylors' children have about their bedroom?
(f) Did the hotel clerk agree at once to change Mr Lee's room?

PRACTICE 1

Fill in the missing words.

A: Hi! Come in and sit down for a minute. I'm going to ring the (1) .... desk. I really must (2) .... about the room they've given me.

B: Oh really? What's the (3) .... with it?

A: Everything! I've (4) .... to get about six drops of water out of the bathroom taps, the toilet won't (5) ...., there's no (6) .... for my razor and it's too hot because the (7) .... doesn't work properly.

B: How much are they charging you?

A: I'm not sure exactly. There's a notice on the door but I think it's (8) ....: it's (9) .... 10 March 1960!

PRACTICE 2

Mr Taylor is going back to the reception desk to see the hotel manager. Practise this dialogue with him before he goes (you are (A)).

A: Can you find out..........?
Mr Taylor: OK, I'll do my best.

> how to turn the water on
> how to make the shower work
> where to collect our letters
> when to get the bus for Palmville
> which way to turn the knobs on the air-conditioner

PRACTICE 3

Saying the same thing with different words: where in the above six dialogues can we use the following words or phrases with no change of meaning?

(a) Do we need to give him a bit extra?
(b) .... isn't valid any more.
(c) I don't think so.
(d) How far must we go?
(e) That's easy!
(f) Surely we can take it ....
(g) I can put it across my legs.
(h) Would you mind changing ....?
(i) I must do one or two things.

PRACTICE 4

In English the tone of the voice rises or falls most on the most important words. In these recorded sentences, which words caused the biggest tone-changes?

(a) According to that notice it's twenty-five.
(b) But look, it's dated July the first.
(c) You're asking too much.
(d) Be careful of that suitcase.

(e) Mind the lid.
(f) You'll soon get used to it.
(g) We are rather full, sir.

PRACTICE 5

What did Mr Taylor say when he went to see the hotel manager? And when he went back to his family?

(a) *Mr Taylor*: Look, ... possibly .... our children's bed? You've given them .... but they need ....
   Manager: I see. What's the number of your ....?
   Mr Taylor: Twelve a and b.
   Manager: No ...., I'll put you in a different one. I'll .... the porter to move your luggage.
(b) *Mrs Taylor*: Well?
   Mr Taylor: I've .... everything .... We're .... to another cottage.

FURTHER STUDY

> The Green Line Taxi Service
> Call 078-2251-9 (8 lines) for a
> prompt, efficient service. 24 hours
> a day. All our taxis are metered and have friendly working drivers.

Notes

metered: The fare is shown on the taxi meter.
working: The driver will help you with luggage, etc.

PRACTICE 6

You telephone a taxi company. The driver won't be able to speak English, but the company will get him to do things for you. How will you pass these requests on?

CAN YOU FIND OUT HOW TO TURN THE WATER ON? 49

(a) Drop you outside the National Bank.
(b) Call at eleven p.m.
(c) Pick you up at the airport at four thirty.
(d) Wait a couple of minutes while you go into a flower shop.
(e) Follow your route on a map that you'll give him.
(f) Change a hundred dinar note.

PRACTICE 7

The Taylors' driver carried one of their cases by putting it on the roof rack. When the Taylors were at their hotel they saw these notices.

SAVE ENERGY
Please turn off all
unnecessary lights.

To call operator
dial 09

(a) How can they save energy?
(b) How can they call the operator?
(c) How can they get the maid to go away?
(d) How can they get the maid to clean the room?

Some hotel information

Important words		
meter	rate	facilities
drop (v.)	de luxe	credit card
pick up	suite	deposit (n.)
tariff	minimum	(in) advance

Hotel Shalimar

721, Sharon Road, Palmville

The Shalimar Hotel, near Palmville, is situated on the site of the ancient capital of Marmar, one hour's drive from the city centre and thirty minutes from Halo international airport.

One hundred and two spacious, luxurious guest rooms and suites, all fully air-conditioned. Each room with private bathroom and shower, radio and colour television.

Our facilities include three restaurants; bar and lounge; two convention and banquet halls; parking for over a hundred cars; tennis courts; souvenir shop; swimming pool; barber shop.

For foreign guests no tax is added to room charge; 10 per cent tax on food and beverages.

For reservations contact your travel agent or our reservation office: Palmville 048-5031/5

1980 TARIFF		
Room Rates (meals not included)		
	Single occupancy	*Double occupancy*
Double	D 150	D 200
Twin De luxe	D 180	D 220
Twin A	D 160	D 210
Twin B	D 150	D 200
Suite		D 400
Meal Rates (minimum charge)		
Breakfast	D 15	
Lunch	D 30	
Dinner	D 35	
Rates subject to change without notice.		

The Diamond Beach Inn
(The Inn closest to Diamond Beach)

Room rates for one or two persons including a full continental breakfast.

Large corner rooms: D 100 per day
Standard rooms: D 85 per day
Small cottage rooms: D 75 per day

Extra guests in room: add 20 dinars per person.

Sorry – No children under ten years.

Minimum 2 days stay at weekend and 3 days over holidays and special events.

Ample 24-hour parking.

Master Charge, Visa and Bank Americard accepted.

Reservations must be secured by your deposit cheque for one night's room rate.

Rates subject to change.

Check-out time: 12 noon.

Notes

the tariff: The list of prices (especially at a hotel).

single occupancy: Occupied by one person.

de luxe: Top class.

a suite: A set of rooms (e.g. bedroom, sitting room and bathroom).

a convention: A conference (especially of businessmen).

a banquet: A formal dinner for a large number of guests.

beverages: Drinks.

subject to change without notice: They may change without warning.

a continental breakfast: This is usually coffee plus some form of bread.

Master Charge, etc: These are credit cards (you pay the credit card company at the end of the month).

a deposit: Money which you pay in advance (before you stay at the hotel).

PRACTICE 8

What answers can you expect when you ring these hotels for information? You are the enquirer (A). Complete the hotel clerk's answers, or your own questions.

(a) *Clerk*: Hotel Shalimar, good morning.
   A: Hello. Can you tell me your rate for a double room, please?
   Clerk: ....?
   A: By one.
   Clerk: Certainly, it's ....
   A: And does that include breakfast?
   Clerk: ....

(b) *Clerk*: Hotel Shalimar, good morning.
   A: Good morning. I'm visiting Palmville next week. How long does it take to the centre of the city from your hotel?
   Clerk: ....

(c) *Clerk*: Hotel Shalimar, good morning.
   A: Hello. I'm trying to arrange a conference for my company. Does your hotel have facilities for large numbers of people?
   Clerk: Oh yes, we have .... We also have ....
   A: How about ....?
   Clerk: There's one in every room, sir, and a radio as well.

(d) *Clerk*: Diamond Beach Inn, good morning.
   A: Hello. I'd like to make a reservation for two nights for myself and my family. Do you take children?
   Clerk: Yes madam, provided that ....

(e) *Clerk*: Diamond Beach Inn, good morning.
   A: I'd like to reserve a large corner room for the nights of May 15th, 16th, and 17th. Mr and Mrs Smith and our son aged twelve Do I need ....?
   Clerk: Yes please sir, ... room rate, that's ....
   A: I believe you ....
   Clerk: Yes sir, we accept three kinds.

PRACTICE 9

You are a member of the hotel staff. How will you reply to a guest who asks these questions?

At the Shalimar
(a) I only had a glass of milk for breakfast, so why can't I pay 50 cents?
(b) Why haven't you added 10 per cent to Mr Smith's room charge? You've added it to mine.

At the Diamond Beach Inn
(c) Why can't we book for Saturday night only?
(d) Why can't I keep my room until 4 pm.?

6 IT SAYS THEY'VE GOT BOATS FOR HIRE

Important words

- unpack
- short (of)
- coat hanger
- picnic
- discover
- electricity
- power cut
- monsoon
- press (v.)
- brochure
- flask
- supermarket
- short cut

During the evening the Taylors' missing suitcase was delivered by the airline. They unpacked it and found they needed more coat hangers. Next day they had breakfast in the open-air restaurant, then walked down some steps to the beach. John wanted to hire a boat but Mrs Taylor wasn't sure if it was safe. However, they found out that the hotel didn't hire out boats any more. Mr Taylor asked the hotel manager about hiring a car and the manager told him there was a car-hire firm just down the road. Mrs Taylor wanted to know about buying things for picnics. They had a refrigerator in their cottage where they could keep food.

Mr Lee ordered breakfast in his room. Later, when he tried to shave, he discovered that there was no electricity. He was told that Palmville often gets power cuts, especially just before the monsoon season. Sometimes the water is cut off as well. Mr Lee went out early with Mr Kay to talk about their book exhibition. Before he went out he left one of his suits for pressing.

DIALOGUE A

Mrs Taylor: Well, I'm glad they discovered our case.
Mr Taylor: So am I. But now we're short of coat hangers. I'll get the maid to bring us some more.
John: Dad, Sarah and I want to hire a boat.
Mrs Taylor: Hire a boat?!
John: Yes, it says in the hotel brochure they've got boats for hire.
Mrs Taylor: You're too young to go out in a boat by yourselves.
John: But Dad can come with us.
Mrs Taylor: I don't know – we must find out if the water's safe.

DIALOGUE B

Mr Lee (on the telephone): Hello, room service?
Clerk: Yes, sir?
Mr Lee: I'd like to order breakfast in my room, please. Shall I give you my order?
Clerk: Yes.
Mr Lee: I'll have a boiled egg, toast and coffee. Oh – and can you tell me whether it's safe to drink the water? I mean water from the tap.
Clerk: Well, we advise you to drink boiled water, sir. The water in your flask is boiled.

DIALOGUE C

Mr Taylor: Excuse me, my son wants to know about hiring a boat.
Manager: We used to hire out boats, sir, but we don't any more. That information's out of date.

Mr Taylor: Ah, that's OK. But could you tell me where I can hire a car?
Manager: There's a car-hire firm just down the road, sir, Kapur Motors. They'll be glad to help you.

DIALOGUE D

Mr Lee (on the telephone): Hello.
Clerk: Yes, can I help you?
Mr Lee: Yes, I want to know why there's no electricity.
Clerk: Sorry sir, there's been a power cut.
Mr Lee: Well, when will it come on again?
Clerk: It's usually off for about half an hour, so we expect it back about eight thirty.

DIALOGUE E

Mr Taylor: I asked about picnic things.
Mrs Taylor: Yes?
Mr Taylor: I was told there's a small supermarket about half a mile down the road.
Mrs Taylor: Let's have a look this evening. It's too hot to walk there now.

DIALOGUE F

Mr Kay: Good morning. Did you sleep well?
Mr Lee: Yes, thanks.
Mr Kay: I hope you don't mind walking to the office. It's not far.
Mr Lee: No, that's fine. I like walking.
Mr Kay: There used to be a short cut behind the hotel but they're digging the road up. How do you like the weather?
Mr Lee: It's certainly warm.
Mr Kay: Yes, we'll be getting rain any day now.

Notes

to hire: Hotels hire out boats to their guests. The guests hire the boats.
a short cut: A short route.

COMPREHENSION QUESTIONS

(a) Why didn't Mrs Taylor want the children to hire a boat?
(b) Why were they unable to hire a boat?
(c) What did Mr Lee find out about the water?
(d) What difficulty did Mr Lee have in the morning?
(e) When was the monsoon expected?

PRACTICE 1

Fill in the missing words.

Here is some information from a (1) .... for hotel guests.

Would guests please note that (2) .... occur from time to time. The (3) .... may be (4) .... for an hour or more.

Guests are advised to drink (5) .... water only. A (6) .... is provided in your room.

(7) ....: cars are available for (8) .... at the hotel. Please apply at the (9) .... desk.

PRACTICE 2

You want to hire a boat, but the old fisherman only speaks Arcanian. An English-speaking Arcanian offers his services. You are the enquirer (A). What did you say?

A: ....
B: Sure, I'll ask him . . . He says yes, and it's fifteen dinars an hour.
A: ....?! But that notice .... Please tell him ....
B: Ten, OK . . . All right, he agrees. Pay in advance, please.
A: One more thing. Could you ask ....?
B: Sure. Yes, he says the bay is quite safe.

PRACTICE 3

You are going on a picnic with a friend. You telephoned him about his plans: you wanted to ask these three questions – 'What time are you planning to leave? How much food are you taking? Are you bringing any ice?' What did you say when his brother (B) answered?

A: Hello? Jack?
B: Yes.
A: Is your brother in?
B: Not yet. He'll be coming in about seven thirty.
A: About the picnic tomorrow. I'd like to know ....
B: All right, but perhaps he ought to phone you himself.
A: OK .... phone me after nine thirty? I'll be out till then.

PRACTICE 4

What does he want to know?

PRACTICE 5

Nowadays Mr Kay works as an agent for Mr Lee's company (and for other publishers as well). Let's ask him what he used to do. Complete his answers.

A: How long have you had this business?
Mr Kay: Since 1977.
A: And what did you do before that?
Mr Kay: I .... for the booksellers, Bugis brothers.

A: Have you always lived in Palmville?
Mr Kay: No, I .... in New Zealand. Then my father sold his business – he .... a chemist's shop – and we came back to Arcania.
A: You've got a nice, new office.
Mr Kay: Yes, it was only built last year. This area .... one of the city markets. Do you see that green building to the left of the harbour?
A: Yes.
Mr Kay: That .... my office.

PRACTICE 6

How did they feel?

(a) When Mrs Taylor said, '..........' she felt very surprised.
(b) Mrs Taylor probably felt happier when Mr Taylor told her that ....
(c) Mr Lee was slightly worried when he was told ....
(d) Mr Lee was rather annoyed when he learned ....

FURTHER STUDY

Talking about the climate. Here is some information from guidebooks to two very different places: the Seychelles (in the Indian Ocean) and Alaska.

Important words

climate	advisable	swimming costume
rainfall	casual(ly)	custom
humid	lightweight	essential
rough	washable	suitable

Seychelles

The lush, green vegetation of these islands was not caused by drought. The annual rainfall is 90 inches, most of which falls during the months of November, December and January.

Since the islands lie outside the cyclone belt, high winds and thunderstorms are rare.

Broadly speaking there are two seasons. The north-west trade winds blow from November to April and this period is hotter and slightly more humid than the remaining months of the year. The south-east trade winds can make the sea somewhat rough from May to October but the slight drop in temperature and the cool winds make a pleasant change.

Climate chart

Climate chart				
Months	Mean temperature C	Humidity %	Rainfall inches	Daily hours of sunshine
January	26.4	83	15	5.7
February	26.9	77	9	6.1
March	26.9	78	10	7.2
April	26.4	80	7	8.1
May	27.7	79	8	8.2
June	26.2	78	4	7.0
July	26.5	81	4	7.4
August	26.4	81	6	7.3
September	26.9	81	6	7.1
October	27.2	83	10	7.1
November	27.4	83	14	7.1
December	27.4	82	14	5.9

What to wear

For women, light cotton dresses, slacks and shorts are advisable at any time of the year. Formal evening dress is seldom worn except at very special functions, as the mood of the islands is to dress casually. A long skirt is popular in the evenings.

Men are most comfortable in slacks with open-neck shirts. All clothing should be lightweight and easily washable.

Swimming costumes are essential, but to observe local custom these should not be worn in town. Sandals are cool but for walking and exploring some of the islands canvas shoes are useful.

Alaska

Climate

Winter temperatures in Anchorage seldom fall below minus 20° F and a typical summer day will be in the high 60s or mid-70s.

Summer days are long, with up to 20 hours of daylight. It gets dark for an hour or two around midnight as the sun dips briefly below the horizon.

Winter days are generally clear and dry. Anchorage receives less snowfall than Cleveland, Ohio.

What to wear

Alaskans believe in comfort and informality. For almost any occasion sports clothes are suitable, although you may want to pack in your suitcase one jacket and tie for evening wear in the city. Bring a raincoat and warm sweater for the autumn and for winter visits you may want a heavy wool or fur coat and gloves. Walking shoes and warm socks are essential.

Notes

the cyclone belt: The area where cyclones (strong circular winds) blow.
trade winds: Winds that blow regularly towards the earth's equator.
mean: Average.
slacks: Trousers (American: pants).
functions: Parties, etc.
20° F: 20° Fahrenheit (−7° Centigrade).

COMPREHENSION QUESTIONS

Seychelles

(a) Which months are the wettest?
(b) What is the average temperature for the year?
(c) When is the sea calmest?
(d) Is a raincoat necessary in July?
(e) Why aren't swimming costumes worn in the town?

Alaska

(f) What is it like in Alaska in the winter?
(g) Does it snow very much in Anchorage in the winter?
(h) What kind of outer clothing is suitable in winter?
(i) Do people like wearing formal clothes?
(j) What is recommended for evening wear?

PRACTICE 7

Fill in the missing words.

In Arcania there are two main (1) ....; one is hot and dry and the other is hot and wet, when the (2) .... reaches 80 per cent and (3) .... reaches 14 inches. During the wettest months of October and November a (4) .... is recommended. (5) .... clothes are suitable all through the year and (6) .... clothing is the rule: formal clothes are only worn for certain evening (7) .... Swimming costumes are essential but please (8) .... local (9) .... and don't wear them in the town.

Important words		
maintain	overseas	telex
mileage	airmail	salesman
member(ship)	quotation	

IT SAYS THEY'VE GOT BOATS FOR HIRE

Coming to Palmville?
Want to rent a car?

We can meet you at the airport or supply you with one of our rental cars anywhere in the country. All our cars are carefully maintained (manual or automatic). Sedans or station wagons.

competitive rates
unlimited mileage
full insurance cover
AAA membership, radio
maps provided free of charge
roof rack available

Special low rates for overseas visitors. Write to us for full details, giving the dates of your visit and we will send by return airmail a quotation and brochure.

Kapur Motors Ltd., 27 West Road, Palmville.
Tel. 052-1478   Telex 927035

Notes

sedans, station wagons: Pictures of the two types of car are shown.
   Another word for 'sedan' is 'saloon'.
manual: The gear lever is moved by hand.
unlimited mileage: You can travel any distance for the same price.
AAA: Arcanian Auto Association.
a quotation: A price offer.

PRACTICE 8

Mr Taylor went to Kapur Motors. What did the salesman say to him?

Mr Taylor: Good morning. I was told you have cars for hire.
Salesman: That's right, sir ....?

64 IT SAYS THEY'VE GOT BOATS FOR HIRE

Mr Taylor: Yes, I'm British.
Salesman: Well, we'll be .... You'll find .... in this brochure. What kind ....?
Mr Taylor: That depends on the price. Maybe one of these small Datsuns. I'll let you know.
Salesman: We're a bit .... at the moment, sir. But you can have a Honda .... overseas visitors.

Sorry – I got lost on the way back.

7 I COULDN'T DRINK ANY MORE, THANKS

Important words		
serve	appointment	shellfish
suggest	snack bar	pie
menu	course	recipe
dish	pretty (adv.)	bill
(in a) hurry	help oneself	settle up

Bill and Jane are a young couple from New Zealand. They were staying in the same hotel as the Taylors; in fact they were neighbours, as they occupied the next cottage. They had arrived a week before the Taylors and knew a restaurant which served good Arcanian food. They suggested going there for a meal, so the four of them went there that evening for dinner. Although they hadn't reserved a table, they managed to get in. There was a long menu with several Arcanian and some western-style dishes and a wine list with some local and some imported wines. Bill was fond of Arcanian wine and persuaded the Taylors to try it.

Mr Lee and Mr Kay were busy with discussions and arrangements for their exhibition. They were short of time for lunch as they had another appointment early in the afternoon, so since they were in a hurry they decided to go to a snack bar.

DIALOGUE A

Mr Taylor: It looks a bit crowded.
Jane: There's a table free in that corner.
Head waiter: Good evening sir.
Mr Taylor: Good evening. We'd like a table for four, please. I'm afraid we don't have a reservation.

DIALOGUE B

Bill: What would you like to drink? Have you tried maki?
Mrs Taylor: Er, no. What's maki?
Bill: The local wine. It's made from mangoes – they drink it with every course.
Mrs Taylor: Is it very strong?
Bill: Quite strong, but you can add water if you like.
Mr Taylor: Let's try it. Shall we order a couple of bottles?

DIALOGUE C

Mr Lee: What do you recommend?
Mr Kay: Have you ever tried squid? How about a squid cutlet?
Mr Lee: It looks like a hamburger.
Mr Kay: It's served in chili sauce, so it's pretty hot.
Mr Lee: OK, I'll try that. Do we help ourselves?
Mr Kay: Sure, self-service here.

DIALOGUE D

Mr Taylor: May I fill your glass?
Jane: Thank you.
Mrs Taylor: I think I'll start with the soup.
Bill: Actually, you finish with the soup in Arcania.
Mrs Taylor: Really?

Mr Taylor: I think I'll have the steak. (to the waiter) I'd like it well done, please.
Waiter: Right, sir.
Jane: The prawn curry's worth trying.
Mrs Taylor: Sorry, I can't eat shellfish. It makes me ill. I think I'd rather have the chicken pie.

DIALOGUE E

Mr Kay: Tea or coffee?
Mr Lee: Coffee for me, please.
Mr Kay: How do you like it? Black or white?
Mr Lee: Black please, one spoonful of sugar. Now, let me pay for all this.
Mr Kay: No, no, it's on me.
Mr Lee: Really?
Mr Kay: Yes, be my guest.

DIALOGUE F

Mr Taylor: Well, it's getting late. Where's the waiter gone?
Bill: He'll be back. He's just bringing another bottle. There he is.
Mrs Taylor: Oh, I couldn't drink any more, thanks.
Jane: That banana pudding was nice. I must get the recipe.
Bill (to the waiter): Sorry, I'm afraid we'll have to cancel that order. Could we have the bill. please.
Waiter: Yes, sir. Would you like separate bills?
Mr Taylor: One bill will do – we'll settle up afterwards.

Notes

squid:
chili: Red pepper.
pretty: Rather.
hot: Spicy, peppery.
help ourselves: Take the food ourselves ('Help yourself to the squid').
well done: Well cooked. The opposite (for steak) is 'rare'. Halfway between is 'medium rare'.
to settle up: To share the cost among each other.

Western-style food: some useful items.

COMPREHENSION QUESTIONS

(a) What did Bill suggest drinking?
(b) How can you make maki less strong?
(c) How does Mr Taylor like his steak?
(d) What did Jane recommend to Mrs Taylor?
(e) What happens if Mrs Taylor eats shellfish?
(f) How does Mr Lee like his coffee?

PRACTICE 1

You have just sat down in a restaurant and you are looking at the menu. Practise this dialogue with your friend (A).

A: What would you like to start with? .... prawn curry?
B: Well, no .... a squid cutlet.

| Would you like |
| How about |
| Have you tried |
| Shall we order |

| I'll have |
| I think I'll have |
| I'd rather have |

PRACTICE 2

How does Jane like her food and drink? Put one word in place of the underlined phrases.

(a) She likes her coffee <u>with milk</u>.
(b) She likes her tea <u>with sugar.</u>
(c) She likes her steak <u>cooked for a very short time.</u>

(d) She likes her curry <u>with plenty of chili in it</u>.
(e) She likes her maki <u>with no water in it</u>.

PRACTICE 3

Conversations in the restaurant. What did the speakers say?

(a) *A*: Now, what do I owe you for the drinks?
    B: It's .... today.
    A: Really? Thanks very much.
(b) *A*: Now let's settle up. What did the hotel cost?
    B: That's all right. Be ....
    A: That's very kind of you. Thanks.
(c) *A*: Could we have a table for four, please?
    B: .... we don't have a table until 8.30, sir.
    A: But .... over there.
    B: Yes sir, but .... that's reserved.
(d) *A*: What's your maki like?
    B: It's a bit sweet and .... strong – too strong for the children, anyway.
(e) *A*: This hamburger's nice.
    B: ...., it isn't hamburger. It's fried squid. .... some more vegetables with it?
(f) *A*: .... I'll have to go. I've got an appointment in my office at two o'clock.
    B: Right. Here comes the waiter.
    A: ...., please, we're in a ....
    Waiter: Yes, sir. Do you want ....?
    A: No, together, please.

PRACTICE 4

Tone-changes on the most important words: where were the main changes of tone in these recorded sentences?

(a) Shall we order a couple of bottles?
(b) I'll try that.
(c) Do we help ourselves?
(d) You finish with the soup in Arcania.
(e) How do you like it?

(f) No, no, it's on me.
(g) Be my guest.
(h) One bill will do.

FURTHER STUDY

> **Important words**
> hospitality superb delicious
> locate(d) overlook atmosphere
> décor

If you love to eat, you'll like the Scala.

'Kotobuki'
Japanese Restaurant

A touch of Japan in the centre of Palmville, Kotobuki offers three dining experiences in the Sushi, Tempura and Tatami rooms, all with the delicate hospitality and tradition of Japan.

Elysée
French Restaurant

Located on the 20th floor, Elysée has an intimate and elegant atmosphere for dining. Exceptional service and traditional French design and décor take you back to France where the art of dining started centuries ago.

'Tao Yuen'
Chinese Restaurant

For a real taste of China walk through the Dragon Gate and treat yourself to the elegance and pleasure of real Chinese cuisine. Superb Pekinese and Cantonese cooking.

Scala Coffee Shop

Located on the second floor, overlooking Independence Square, the Coffee Shop offers quick, light meals and delicious coffee at any time of the day in a pleasant atmosphere.

I COULDN'T DRINK ANY MORE, THANKS 71

Notes

décor: Interior decoration.
cuisine: Cooking.

PRACTICE 5

Two friends, (A) and (B), are talking about lunch. Complete their conversation.

A: Where shall we go for lunch? What about the Scala?
B: OK, but which restaurant?
A: They say the .... is .... trying.
B: Actually, I'd .... go there. Heights .... me ....
A: All right, then. What do you suggest?
B: Well, I'm in a bit of a hurry, so why don't we go ....?

PRACTICE 6

A short 'Thank You' letter. Fill in the missing words from the last Important Words box.

Dear Fatima,
Many thanks for the (1) .... lunch last Tuesday. I enjoyed meeting so many interesting people in such a pleasant (2) .... I had never been to an Arabian restaurant before and I thought the (3) .... was beautiful. And the food was (4) .... I hope I can return the (5) .... soon.

Yours,
  Sandra

What's on the menu?

Important words	
flavour (v.)	celebrate
selection	dessert
tropical	cocktail
home-made	basement

FAT SAM'S

Appetisers

Crown Dinner   D 35

Mussels
Cooked in their shells
with butter and garlic.   D 8

Sam's special selection
(prepared at your table)

Surprise Omelette
Choice of mushroom,
anchovy, ham or fine herbs,
made with fresh eggs.   D 5

Cinnamon Steak
Prime steak grilled in butter
and served with a spiced
sauce.

Sashimi
Delicious raw seafood
Japanese style.   D 8

King Prawns
Deep fried in crisp, golden
batter.

Shrimp Salad
Salad of fresh shrimps
served with choice of
dressing.   D 3.50

Salad
Lettuce, young corn, green
and red peppers, served with
French or Thousand Isle
dressing.

Are you celebrating a
special event? Birthday or
Anniversary?

Vegetables
A selection of freshly cooked
vegetables is included with
the main course.

We will prepare our
special dessert for
D 5 per person.

Let your waitress know
when ordering dinner.

Rice
Sam's special fried rice
or plain boiled rice.

Dessert
A selection of fresh, tropical
fruit.
Tea or coffee.

Oriental tropical drinks
Complete cocktail selection
available.

Plum Wine
A glass of fragrant home-
made plum wine.

'Only your steak gets more attention than you do'.

I COULDN'T DRINK ANY MORE, THANKS 73

Take home the delicious taste of Hotel Scala

Many of the fine foods you've enjoyed in our fabulous restaurants are now available through our take-away stores. Home-made sausages, cold cuts and breads at the Scala Delicatessen and delicious cakes, pies and ice creams at the Patisserie – both located at basement level.

Notes

appetisers: Snacks to start your meal.

batter: A covering made of flour, eggs, water, etc. for things that you fry.

dressing: Sauce for a salad.

cocktail: A special mixed drink.

cold cuts: Cold cooked meats ready for cutting.

a delicatessen: A shop where rather special or unusual foods are sold.

a patisserie: A shop for rather special cakes.

PRACTICE 7

More talk about eating out.

(a) It's your wife's birthday. What will you ask the waitress at Fat Sam's to do?
(b) You want your guests to take food from the table. What do you say?
(c) 'From chicken, herbs and white wine'.
   What was the question?
(d) 'Well done, please'.
   What was the question?
(e) Finish (B)'s answer.
   A: Will you have the fried rice?
   B: No, I'd ....
(f) Someone offered Mrs Taylor the mussels. What did she reply?
(g) What did (B) say?
   A: Hey, where's our waiter gone?
   B: He'll .... He forgot the salad dressing.

(h) What did (B) say?
   A: I like the food at the Scala delicatessen. It's always so fresh.
   B: That's because ....
(i) Someone asks the way to
   the patisserie at the Scala. What will
   you answer? (look at the sketch).
   Go .... and ....
   to ....

8 WE'D BETTER LOOK AT THE MAP AGAIN

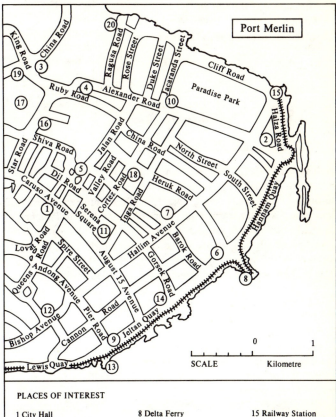

PLACES OF INTEREST

1 City Hall
2 City Bus Terminal
3 Public Library
4 Museum and Art Gallery
5 Mariam Temple
6 Tourist Information Office
7 Police Headquarters
8 Delta Ferry
9 Jeltan Quay
10 Roman Catholic Cathedral
11 National Memorial
12 Friday Mosque
13 Kerman Pier
14 General Hospital
15 Railway Station
16 Chinok Stadium
17 Supreme Court
18 Botanical Gardens
19 Zoo
20 Plato University

Important words		
museum	one-way street	branch
art gallery	staff	driving licence
headquarters	salary	wallet
stadium	campus	librarian
scale (n.)	assistant	excursion
right-hand drive	secretary	boring
lane	parallel	invitation card
traffic lights	turning	association
statue	speed limit	block (n.)
fine (n.&v.)	overtake	guide (n.)
offence		

The Taylors in their hired car went to have a look at Port Merlin. They hired a small Honda – right-hand drive because in Arcania you drive on the left. Driving wasn't easy: the traffic went very fast where there weren't traffic jams, it moved from lane to lane and it was often difficult to see the traffic lights and road signs. They wanted especially to look at Mariam Temple which is famous for its statues. On the way to the Temple they were fined for a traffic offence. A policeman waved them down and told Mr Taylor he had to pay an 'on the spot' fine for driving the wrong way down a one-way street. Mr Taylor decided not to argue about it.

In Palmville, Mr Lee and Mr Kay paid a visit to Plato University which was a customer of Mr Lee's company. The University library had given him some good orders in recent years. On the way Mr Kay called at his bank as he wanted to draw some money out of his account to pay his staff salaries (he had a very small staff – an assistant and a secretary). Plato University has another campus in Port Merlin, in Ragusa Road, which runs parallel to Rose Street near the north shore.

DIALOGUE A

Mr Taylor: OK, let's stop a minute, we'd better look at the map again. Right, now we're here, just past Serena Square.

Mrs Taylor: So we keep straight on along Caruso Avenue, turn right at the City Hall, then take the second turning on the left.

Mr Taylor: I wonder if you can park there.
John: I've seen one or two parking meters.
Mr Taylor: All of you, keep an eye on the street names.
Sarah: Watch the speed limit, Dad. Forty kilometres an hour it says. And no overtaking.

DIALOGUE B

Mr Kay: There's a car park by the main branch but not here, so I'll park in that side street and go on on foot. I won't be long – I'll be about ten minutes.
Mr Lee: OK, I'll look after the car. Are we allowed to park here?
Mr Kay: I think so; anyway, I can't see any 'no parking' signs.

DIALOGUE C

Policeman: This is a one-way street. Didn't you see the sign?
Mr Taylor: Sorry, no, I didn't.
Policeman: May I see your driving licence?
Mr Taylor: Yes, it's an international one.
Policeman: OK . . . Well, that'll be twenty dinars.
Mr Taylor: Eh?
Policeman: The fine. It's twenty dinars.

DIALOGUE D

Mr Kay: This is Miss Sorak, the chief librarian.
Miss Sorak: How do you do?
Mr Lee: How do you do? You have a fine library. Have you been working here long?
Miss Sorak: For about two years. Have you just arrived in Palmville?
Mr Lee: Yes, the day before yesterday.

DIALOGUE E

Mr Taylor: The place is full.
Mrs Taylor: You saw all those coaches. It's obviously an excursion.
Mr Taylor: How about visiting the museum first?

Sarah: Can't we go to the beach? Museums are so boring.
Mrs Taylor: Oh shut up. You'll have plenty of time for swimmimg.

DIALOGUE F

Miss Sorak: I was interested to hear about your exhibition. How long does it stay open?
Mr Lee: Ten days. I do hope you'll come to the opening.
Miss Sorak: Of course. Mr Kay sent me an invitation card last week.
Mr Kay: You know where it is, don't you?
Miss Sorak: The Publishers Association? Oh yes, in the block opposite the National Museum.

Notes

Botanical Gardens: Gardens where rare plants are grown.
a lane: Traffic is kept in separate lanes by painted lines.
a campus: A university area.
a parking meter: A meter which shows you how long you have parked.
to overtake: To pass (in a vehicle).
an excursion: A tour by a group of people. It often has a guide who leads them.
I do hope: 'Do' is used for emphasis and politeness.
a block: A large, square building.

COMPREHENSION QUESTIONS

(a) Does the traffic always move fast in Port Merlin?
(b) What was Mr Taylor's traffic offence?
(c) What was the connection between Mr Lee and Plato University?
(d) Was Mr Kay's account at the main branch of the bank?
(e) Where did he park his car?
(f) How much was Mr Taylor fined?
(g) What does Sarah think about museums?
(h) Will Miss Sorak be coming to the exhibition?
(i) Where will the exhibition take place?

PRACTICE 1

Fill in the missing words.

We went on an (1) .... by coach last week and the driver was (2) .... twice for traffic (3) .... As we were passing the Art (4) .... a policeman waved us down and told the driver that he had gone over the (5) .... He told the driver to pay the (6) .... on the spot. Later, the driver went by mistake through the (7) .... when they were red. Another policeman stopped the driver and asked to see his (8) ....

PRACTICE 2

Practise this dialogue with the driver (B).

A: Didn't you notice the sign?
B: No, I'm sorry, what sign?
A: That one over there. It says ....
B: Sorry, I didn't notice it. I had the sun in my eyes.

> No right turn
> No parking
> Lorries prohibited
> Keep in lane
> No overtaking

PRACTICE 3

How had the driver (see Practice 2) broken the law?

(a) By .... where it wasn't allowed.
(b) By ....
(c) By ....
(d) By not ....
(e) By ....

PRACTICE 4

You are a policeman on duty outside Port Merlin railway station and you are asked the way by several drivers. How will you tell them to reach these places (mention distances):

(a) Mariam Temple.
(b) The Roman Catholic Cathedral.
(c) The General Hospital.
(d) Kerman Pier.
(e) The Botanical Gardens.
(f) Plato University.

FURTHER STUDY

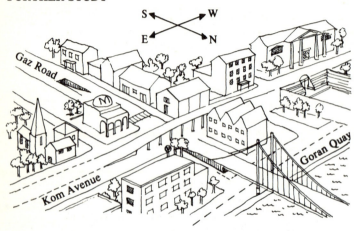

PRACTICE 5

> **Important words**
> flyover
> U-turn
> pedestrian crossing
> underpass

What did the people say to each other in their cars? Complete their conversations (in this city they drive on the right).

(a) (They are driving west along Kom Avenue and want to turn into Gaz Road for the underpass.)
   A: You'd .... stay in the right-hand .... Otherwise we'll be ....

B: OK. Are we allowed to make a ....?
A: Yes, there's a .... by those trees.

(b) (They are going south over the bridge.)
A: I've got to .... Peter up at the entrance to the metro.
B: Which entrance?
A: The one on Kom Avenue.
B: But it says ....
A: So what can I do?
B: Why not stop for a few minutes on Gaz Road at the end of the ....? I can run across and get him. I .... long.

(c) (They are going east along Goran Quay.)
A: That's the bridge ahead of us. How do we get on to it?
B: Take the .... after the bridge, then do a .... on to the bridge. But don't take the ...., otherwise we'll be going west along Kom Avenue.

(d) (They are going north along Gaz Road and have almost reached the entrance to the underpass.)
A: I wonder if .... here? I want to go back the way we came.
B: Good Lord, no, not yet – you can't do a .... in front of the .... We'll have to go on to Goran Quay and turn under the bridge. And look out for ice. The road may be slippery there.

(e) (They are going west along Goran Quay.)
A: We can't stop on the quay, there's a .... sign.
B: Well, I'll have to .... the bank, otherwise I shan't be able to pay the staff .... tomorrow. So I'm going to turn left into that ....

Here is an item from a newspaper about traffic conditions in Singapore.

Important words	
district	vehicle
ambulance	owner
fire engine	suburbs
exempt	outskirts

Policewomen in uniform with stickers in their hands are looking closely at sedans and taxis in downtown districts in the morning rush-hour to see if any of them are heading for the 'restricted zone' with less than 4 passengers (including the driver).

All sedans and taxis are required to enter the city centre with all their seats occupied. If not, and if they have no ticket, they are subject to fines of $50 each time they are checked.

The restricted zone designated by the government is about 6.2 square kilometres. The law aims at curbing congestion of vehicles in the central business district, thus making it easier for cars and city buses to flow, as well as reducing air pollution in the centre. Private sedans have to get a $4 entrance ticket when they fail to carry four riders. Sedans used by the head of state, cargo trucks, ambulances, fire engines and sedans occupied by foreign diplomats, however, are exempt from the scheme.

The policewomen at check-points do not stop offending vehicles on the spot, but record their licence numbers and send stickers to their owners later. Parking charges in the city centre are higher than those in the suburbs.

Fifteen large parking buildings were built on the outskirts of the city to accommodate cars whose drivers do not want to come into the central zone by car. Special bus services are available.

By building circular roads outside and around the restricted zone the authorities made it possible for drivers to reach their destinations without passing through the busy downtown districts.

Notes

stickers: Labels with a special message which can be stuck on to something.
downtown: Central.
$: Dollars.
offending vehicles: Vehicles which break the law.

PRACTICE 6

(A) is a newspaper reporter who is interested in Singapore's 'restricted zone' scheme for traffic. (B) is a city government employee. (A) asked several questions beginning 'What happens if .... ?' (B) gave these answers. What were (A)'s questions?

(a) *A*: ....?
   B: They're fined $50 each time.
(b) *A*: ....?
   B: Then they don't have to pay the fine.
(c) *A*: ....?
   B: They don't have to pay because they're exempt from the scheme.
(d) *A*: ....?
   B: They send stickers to their owners.
(e) *A*: ....?
   B: They can use parking buildings on the city outskirts and travel into the centre by special buses.
(f) *A*: ....?
   B: They can use the circular roads.

PRACTICE 7

(a) 'Are you the owner of this vehicle?'
A policeman asked Mr Lee this question while he was waiting in the side street for Mr Kay. What was Mr Lee's reply?

(b)
Why is it especially difficult for the driver of this car to overtake?

PRACTICE 8

Some road signs. (A) hasn't seen them. (B) has. What do the signs say – how does (B) answer (A)'s questions?

(a) *A*: Why can't we walk along the bridge?
(b) *A*: Why can't we ride on the motorway?
(c) *A*: Why can't I turn here?
(d) *A*: Why do we have to turn right?
(e) *A*: Is it still one-way traffic?
(f) *A*: Why are we slowing down?

PRACTICE 9

```
Thursday    August 8


6.30 — Drinks party
              at home
```

```
Thursday    August 8


6.30 — Book exhibition
       ( Publishers
         Association )
```

Two appointments diaries. The page on the right is from Miss Sorak's diary. The page on the left is from her friend's (A). Complete the conversation between them.

A: I'm having ………. on ………. I ………. come.
Miss Sorak: Thanks very much. I'm ………. at 6.30 because I've got ………. at the ………. for ………. but I'd ………. later if that's all right.
A: Yes, of course.

9 CAN I HAVE ONE MADE TO MEASURE?

Important words		
menswear	old-fashioned	style
satisfied	bargain (v.)	pattern
fitting (n.)	afford	come/take to pieces
measurements	bazaar	fixed
souvenir	run out (of)	awful
department store	spare (adj.)	suit (v.)
design (n.)	sold out	calculator
shape (v.)	try on	wrap up

Mr Lee had heard that clothes were cheaper in Arcania than in his own country so he had a look inside a menswear shop. He decided to have a safari jacket made as he wasn't satisfied with the ready-made ones, although they were his size. The shop assistant told him they could have it ready within four days and asked him to come for a fitting the following day. When he went back for the fitting some of the measurements weren't quite right.

The Taylors went shopping for souvenirs in Port Merlin. First they went to a department store where they asked about some silver-plated candle holders of a rather unusual design: they were shaped like old-fashioned ships. Mrs Taylor tried to bargain but the shop assistant told her that she couldn't reduce the price. In the end they decided they couldn't afford them. In the bazaar they looked at a stall with rolls of silk for sale. Mrs Taylor wanted some silk to make a dress. After changing her mind several times she decided on dark blue. Meantime Mr Taylor went to buy some film for his camera. He had run out of film because he had forgotten to bring his spare films with him. But the shop had sold out of his type of colour film.

DIALOGUE A

Shop assistant: Can I help you?
Mr Lee: I was just looking at these safari jackets.
Shop assistant: This one looks like your size, sir. Would you like to try it on?
Mr Lee: OK. Yes, I like the colour, but I'm not sure about the style. Can I have one made to measure, maybe in a lighter brown? I suppose you have some patterns?
Shop assistant: Of course, sir. Do you like this material? It's a cotton-polyester mixture, very hard-wearing.

DIALOGUE B

Mrs Taylor: Those are rather attractive, aren't they?
Mr Taylor: Yes, what are they for?
Shop assistant: They're candle holders.
Mrs Taylor: How much are they?
Shop assistant: Six hundred dinars the pair, madam.
Mrs Taylor: Can you sell them separately?
Shop assistant: Sorry, madam, only as a pair.
Mr Taylor: But how would we get them home? Do they come to pieces?
Shop assistant: Yes, you can take them to pieces like this . . . and you can easily fit them together again.

Mrs Taylor: Could you give us some discount on that price?
Shop assistant: I'm afraid not, madam, our prices are fixed.

DIALOGUE C

Mrs Taylor: It's one metre wide, so for a dress I'll need, let's see, four metres.
Mr Taylor: How do you like the green?
Mrs Taylor: Oh no, I look awful in green.
Sarah: I think blue suits you best, Mum.
Mrs Taylor: Yes . . . well, I think I'll take the light blue, no, on second thoughts I prefer the dark blue. It'll go better with my new shoes.

DIALOGUE D

Shopkeeper: Are you being served, sir?
Mr Lee: I'm just looking, thanks.
Shopkeeper: Can I interest you in these pocket calculators?
Mr Lee: That depends on the price.
Shopkeeper: They're very good value, only a hundred and five dinars including the case. Would you like me to show you how it works?
Mr Lee: Well, not just now, thanks – I'll let you know.

DIALOGUE E

Mr Taylor: Do you sell colour film for slides?
Shopkeeper: No sir, only for prints. We're out of stock at the moment but we'll be getting some in this afternoon.
Mr Taylor: Thanks, I'll call back sometime tomorrow. I'll just take these postcards for now.
Shopkeeper: Right, shall I wrap them up for you?
Mr Taylor: Yes please. What time do you open tomorrow?
Shopkeeper: Nine o'clock, sir.

DIALOGUE F

Mr Lee: OK, but the sleeves need to be about half an inch longer.
Shop assistant: I'll see to it, sir.

Mr Lee: And could you make it fit a bit more loosely under the arms?

Shop assistant: A bit looser, all right. And did you decide about the lining?

Mr Lee: Yes, I'd like it half-lined.

Notes

silver-plated: Covered with a thin layer of silver.

a department store: A big store with many departments where various things are sold.

sold out of: In this verb phrase the verb 'sell' is almost always in the past tense.

polyester: A man-made material.

hard-wearing: You can wear it for a long time before it wears out.

a shopkeeper: This suggests the owner, or manager, of a shop.

a calculator: A small machine for solving mathematical problems.

a slide: A transparent photograph.

COMPREHENSION QUESTIONS

(a) Why wasn't Mr Lee satisfied with the ready-made jackets?
(b) What was wrong with the sleeves when he had the fitting?
(c) What did the shop assistant show Mr Taylor how to do?
(d) Why didn't Mrs Taylor choose green silk?
(e) How many square metres of silk did she buy?

PRACTICE 1

Fill in the missing words in these advertisements.

For Sale

Men's shirts, military (1) .... in hard-wearing (2) .... cotton material. Colours: white, light blue, khaki. All (3) .... £4.50 each. £8.50 a (4) ....

Pictures you will be proud of! Send us your favourite colour (5) .... and we will make beautiful (6) .... from them. £0.50 for 4 inches by 3.

Rota Brothers (7) .... store announces its grand winter sale, commencing January 7 until 12th. 5–15% (8) .... on all marked prices.

Garden walls made to your own (9) .... Blocks in various (10) .... (triangular, star- (11) ...., etc.). At prices you can (12) ....

PRACTICE 2

Which sentences or phrases in the dialogue mean:

(a) I've changed my mind.
(b) We haven't any now.
(c) Wouldn't you like to buy . . .?
(d) How do you use them?
(e) Could you make it cheaper?
(f) I haven't decided to buy anything yet.

PRACTICE 3

Practise this dialogue with the shop assistant (B).

A: Could I ....?
B: Right, OK.
A: And when will it/they be ready?
B: Let's see, today's Tuesday – Friday afternoon after three.

> have this suit cleaned
> have these shirts washed
> have this watch repaired
> get these trousers pressed
> have some prints made

PRACTICE 4

Practise the following dialogues again but talk about these articles (make changes as necessary):

Dialogue A:	an anorak	a tracksuit
Dialogue B:	table lamps	ashtrays

Dialogue D: cassette recorders portable television sets
Dialogue E: batteries for a radio refills for a pen

PRACTICE 5

(a) If the candle holders are in a sale and the shop is offering 10 per cent off, what will the assistant say to Mrs Taylor?
(b) You are having a shirt made but it doesn't fit you. The sleeves are too long and the collar is too tight. What will you say to the shopkeeper?

FURTHER STUDY

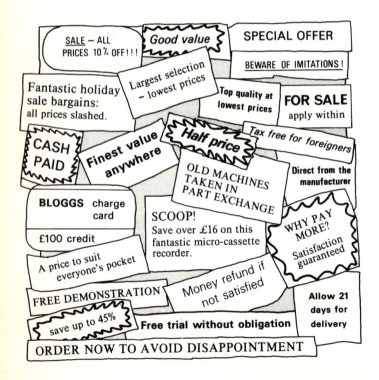

PRACTICE 6

Which of the above advertisements means:

(a) Try it – you can return it to us if you don't like it.
(b) We make them and sell them ourselves.
(c) You're sure to like it. It isn't worth paying extra.
(d) We'll show you how it works – there's no charge.
(e) If you don't like it you can have your money back.
(f) We pay you on the spot.
(g) You'll be sorry if you don't get one now.
(h) Anyone can afford it.

Important words
value (v.&n.)
obligation
part-exchange
 (v.&n.)
quality

Yes – it's a hundred dinars off yesterday's price increase.

Sell us your old Persian Carpet

It may be worth more than you think. We will value your old Persian carpet without charge and without obligation. Then if you wish we will purchase it from you or, if you prefer, part-exchange it for another of your choice. We will give you very good prices, particularly for fine pieces, but whatever the quality and even if a little worn yours may still be worth more than you think.

We are specialists in this field and whether you wish to sell or exchange you will always find us helpful and fair. Call us for advice without obligation.

Kashgai Brothers, Jeltan Quay, Port Merlin, Tel . . .

Notes

fine pieces: Fine examples (of carpets).

PRACTICE 7

(A) has just rented a new flat. He is telling his friend about the new carpet that he bought. Finish what he said. Some words are given to help you.

A: You know that old Persian carpet we had in our flat in Gerbil Road? Well . . .

asked them
to value,
for cash

Mr Kashgai,
a little worn,
fair price

suggested
taking,
in part-
exchange

my wife
thinks,
goes well
with

What are the customer's rights?

Important words	
goods	product
second-hand	defect (n.)
hire-purchase	grateful
faulty	

Notes

goods: Things for sale, things bought.
aren't obliged: Aren't required by law.
second-hand: Already used.
hire-purchase: When you buy something on hire-purchase you pay for it gradually e.g. month by month.
warranty: Guarantee. New goods are usually under warranty.

PRACTICE 8

(A) knows something about sales law. His friends and relations often ask him for advice. What does he tell them?

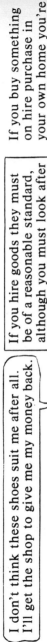

> I don't think these shoes suit me after all. I'll get the shop to give me my money back.
>
> Shops aren't obliged to give you your money back if you simply decide you don't like the goods.

> If you hire goods they must be of a reasonable standard, although you must look after them properly.

> If you buy something on hire purchase in your own home you're allowed a few days to change your mind.

> If you didn't order the goods you don't have to pay for them.

> A spring has come through the seat. What protection do you have if second-hand goods are faulty? See Sale of Goods Act, 1893.

Limited Warranty

This product is warranted for six (6) months from the date of purchase against electrical and mechanical defects in material and workmanship. If the unit fails to operate during the period return it postage prepaid to Electric Service Station, Hoburg, Mississippi 50321 for repair or replacement without charge at the manufacturer's option.

(a) B: You know that blouse I bought last week.
   A: Yes.
   B: Well, I've decided I don't like it. It doesn't go with my green skirt so I think I'll ask the shop for my money back.
   A: Ah, but ……….
   B: Oh.
   A: But if you haven't worn it, you can ask the shop ……….
(b) C: You know those books I wanted.
   A: Yes.
   C: Well, look what they've sent me.
   A: I see. So you didn't order these titles.
   C: No.
   A: In that case ……….
(c) D: I was thinking of buying one of those television sets, you know, the new colour portable, but they're pretty expensive.
   A: Why don't you ……….
   D: That depends how big the payments are.
(d) E: There's something wrong with that new cassette recorder I bought.
   A: Is it still ……….?
   E: Yes, it's only two months old.
   A: So you'd better………. to the ………. and he'll either ………. Tell them about the ………. in a separate letter.
   E: What'll it cost?
   A: Nothing, they'll do it ………. But you'll have to pay ……….

PRACTICE 9

A short letter of complaint. (A) has bought the second-hand sofa in the picture above. She telephoned the seller about it but the seller wasn't very helpful. Can you finish (A)'s letter?

                      21 Oak Road
                      New Town
                      21 January 1980

Dear Sir,
With regard to the ………. which I bought from you last week I have noticed the following ……….

When I sat on it a .... because the cloth was ....

I have .... it .... and I shall be grateful to receive from you the amount of the enclosed bill.

Yours faithfully,
....

10 WE COULD SEE THEM DOING THE FLOWER DANCE

Important words

folk	join in	interval
handicraft	procession	pity (n.)
display (n.)	team	complimentary
show (n.)	concert	programme
traditional	orchestra	hold on (to)
dress (n.)	performance	let go (of)
poster	audience	festival
spectator	pottery	harvest

Just outside Port Merlin there is an Arcanian Folk Village, a place where you can see displays of traditional Arcanian sports and customs. The Taylors visited it one afternoon. It was surrounded by a high wooden fence and inside there were all kinds of Arcanian buildings, some with tiled roofs, some with thatched roofs. The people looking after them and working in them wore Arcanian dress. Many of them spoke English. There were posters advertising all kinds of events. When they went to see some Arcanian dancing Mrs Taylor and some of the other spectators were invited to join in. Later, the Taylors waited to see an Arcanian wedding procession passing by (this was part of the reconstruction of the traditional Arcanian arranged marriage) but they failed to get near it. They also missed the elephant race – this is between two teams of elephants and their riders but it doesn't take place very often. They talked about their visit later with Bill and Jane at the hotel.

In Palmville Mr Lee went to the National Theatre to hear a concert by the Palmville Symphony Orchestra. The performance started at seven o'clock and as they were busy with appointments Mr Lee and Mr Kay had no time for dinner, but they managed to get a snack in the bar during the interval. The audience wasn't very large, in fact the theatre was only three-quarters full.

DIALOGUE A

Mr Taylor: What's this place?
Mrs Taylor: It says 'Arcanian handicrafts' – see, all sorts of pottery and things made of brass.
Sarah: Dad, can we see the puppet show?
Mr Taylor: Where's that?
Sarah: It says it's in the little theatre – you know, we passed it on the way in.
Mrs Taylor: We can't, Sarah, look, two thirty. It started half an hour ago.
Mr Taylor: What a pity.
Mrs Taylor: If we went to the main square we could see some Arcanian dancing. We could see them doing the flower dance.
Mr Taylor: That's a good idea.

DIALOGUE B

Mr Kay: How would you like to hear a concert this evening?
Mr Lee: I'd like to very much.
Mr Kay: Only a friend of mine promised he'd get me some complimentary tickets. The concert hall's not far from here – we could go there straight after work.
Mr Lee: Who's playing?

Mr Kay: It's the Palmville Symphony Orchestra – they're doing an eighteenth-century programme.

DIALOGUE C

Dancer: Hold on to my belt.
Mrs Taylor: Like this?
Dancer: Yes, now we move four steps forward . . . good, and two sideways. That's right. Now let go of my belt and we all turn to face in the opposite direction.
John: Well done, Mum.
Mrs Taylor: What do I do now?
Dancer: Now we all advance to the middle of the circle and pick a flower. Hold the flowers up so that they touch.

DIALOGUE D

Mr Lee: Wasn't that the bell?
Mr Kay: Yes, it's time to go back. What did you think of the first half, then?
Mr Lee: Not bad at all, I thought. I reckon they played the Vivaldi best.
Mr Kay: Yes, the soloist was trained abroad. In fact he's just come back from another tour in the United States.

DIALOGUE E

Mrs Taylor: What's happened to the procession?
Sarah: I saw them carrying the bride. She was in a sort of chair supported on wooden poles.
John: I saw them coming down that hill.
Mr Taylor: This is a waste of time. I reckon they've gone the other way.
Mrs Taylor: Very likely.

DIALOGUE F

Mrs Taylor: It's a pity we didn't see the elephant race.
Mr Taylor: Yes, that was bad luck, but they only have it every other week.

Bill: You know, if you stayed on a few extra days you'd see the lantern festival.

Jane: Oh yes, that's well worth seeing. Some friends of ours saw it last year. They celebrate the harvest by hanging lanterns in the trees.

Mr Taylor: Ah well, we can't manage that. We've already got our flight bookings.

Notes

a reconstruction: An imitation.

an arranged marriage: A marriage arranged by the parents of the bride and bridegroom.

only: This is an introductory use of 'only'. It has a meaning similar to 'because'.

complimentary tickets: The tickets were bought and then presented as a gift.

a soloist: A single player or singer who performs with an orchestra at a concert.

to stay on: To stay longer.

COMPREHENSION QUESTIONS

(a) How did Sarah know about the puppet show?
(b) What did Mrs Taylor do at the dancing?
(c) Do you think the procession was for a real wedding?
(d) How many times a month does the elephant race take place?
(e) Do the elephants race alone?
(f) Did Mr Kay have to pay for his concert tickets?
(g) How did Mrs Taylor know what to do in the dance?
(h) Do you think the concert was popular?
(i) Why won't the Taylors manage to see the lantern festival?

PRACTICE 1

Fill in the missing words in this extract from 'What's on in Palmville This Week'.

	Mon	Tues	Wed	Thurs	Fri	Sat	Sun
							1
September	☐2	☐3	4	5	6	7	8
	9	10	11	12	13	14	15
	16	17	18	19	20	21	22
	23	24	25	26	27	28	29
	30						

☐ = Public Holiday

Monday, September 2

Special event: Lantern (1) .... Lantern (2) .... in Arcanian dress starts from City Square at 7.00 pm. (3) .... are asked not to bring their cars.

(4) .... exhibition: Arcanian blue clay (5) .... and silverware, Young People's Gallery, Orange Grove Road. For fuller details see page nineteen.

Arcanian (6) .... painting: A special lecture on the methods and materials of Arcanian painting, fifteenth-nineteenth centuries. At the (7) .... Village, Bando Gardens.

207th (8) .... of the National Symphony (9) .... (10) ....: Overture 'Fidelio' (Beethoven), Clarinet Concerto in A (Mozart), Symphony No. 1 in E (Sibelius).

Fashion (11) ....: A (12) .... of Arcanian (13) .... in silk and hand-printed cotton. Refreshments will be served during the (14) .... Admission: D10 including refreshments.

PRACTICE 2

Practise this dialogue with Mrs Taylor.

Mrs Taylor: What's on this afternoon?

A: Let's have a look at the poster . . . Well, if we went to the main square we could..........

> see some dancing
> see some people dancing
> see them doing the flower dance
> hear them playing some music

PRACTICE 3

Which phrases or sentences are missing in the dialogues below (you can find them in Dialogues A–F).

(a) *A*: I can't eat all this.
    B: What about taking the rest away in a bag?
    A: Yes, ...!
(b) *A*: Is there a toilet anywhere?
    B: Yes, I saw one ....
    A: What, near the entrance?
    B: That's right.
(c) *A*: I'm afraid we can't get a booking – the flight's full.
    B: ....
(d) *A*: This is your horse.
    B: OK.
    A: Now, ... the rope. Don't .... or he'll run away.
(e) *A*: There's a flower show tomorrow at the National Theatre. Do you want to go?
    B: I'd ....
(f) *A*: Well, I managed to pass the exam.
    B: ....
(g) *A*: ....?
    B: Take the bottle with both hands and pass it to the person on your left.
(h) *A*: What did you think of the puppet show?
    B: .... The puppets looked quite real.
(i) *A*: I'm afraid I didn't pass the exam.
    B: Really? That .... Better luck next time.
(j) *A*: Are you going there for Christmas?
    B: Yes, we are.
    A: .... you could be there for the New Year.
    B: It's worth thinking about. How do .... the New Year there?
    A: By wearing new clothes, giving presents and so on.

PRACTICE 4

Find phrases or sentences in the Dialogues which suggest that the speaker:

(a) Agrees that something has probably happened.
(b) Recommends something strongly.
(c) Says that something can't be done.
(d) Is bored and wants to leave.
(e) Wants to know the correct way to do something.
(f) Is looking for something but can't see it.
(g) Is sorry (because they didn't see something).

PRACTICE 5

(B)'s wife telephones him at the office. What are the two missing words in their conversation?

A: Hello dear, are you still busy?
B: A bit. Why?
A: ………. the Browns are leaving in half an hour. They're going ………. to the airport.
B: OK, one more phone call and I'll leave ………. afterwards.

PRACTICE 6

Tone-changes on the most important words. Which were the important words in these recorded sentences?

(a) Can we see the puppet show?
(b) How would you like to hear a concert this evening?
(c) What do I do now?
(d) You'd see the lantern festival.
(e) We've already got our flight bookings.

FURTHER STUDY

Here is an extract from a city entertainment guide.

Important words	
entertainment	
amusement	tennis court
attraction	equipment

Cinemas

The principal ones, showing English-language films, are the Regal and the Majestic in Gulf Road and the Ocean and the Hollywood in Juno Avenue. Arcanian films (in Arcanian) are shown at the Paris, Sky and Crystal theatres. Seats cost D 3.50 to D 10.00 and it is advisable to book in advance. The last performance is usually at 9.30 p.m.

Nightclubs

One of the best is the Golden Squid (32 Gulf Road), also the Miramar which has exotic Chinese décor and regular cabaret shows. The approximate price for an evening's entertainment at one of these clubs would be D 50 to D 90 per person excluding drinks.

Goluk Amusement Centre

Principal attractions are the funfair and the theatre showing Arcanian opera. There are also tennis courts and an ice-skating rink (equipment can be hired). Admission is D 2.50 (half price for children).

Notes

a cabaret: A show by dancers, etc., at a nightclub or expensive restaurant.

a funfair: A collection of amusements, usually places for playing games, machines for riding in, etc.

equipment: Things which are used for a special activity (e.g. rackets for tennis).

a rink: A round area for skating (on ice-skates or on wheels).

PRACTICE 7

Two friends (A) and (B) have a free day. They are deciding what to do with their spare time. Complete their conversation.

A: If we (1) .... to the Regal we (2) .... that new film 'Superman'.

B: I've seen it, I'm afraid. How (3) .... to see an Arcanian film?

A: Well, my Arcanian isn't very good. I (4) ....n't understand very much. But how much (5) .... if we (6) .... to a night club this evening?

B: Let's see – there's the Golden Squid, of course, but that'll be expensive. If we (7) .... there it (8) .... at least fifty dinars each. And if we (9) .... a few drinks it (10) .... even more.

A: Maybe we'd (11) .... go to the amusement centre.

B: Right. At least it (12) .... very much to go in.

A: And if we (13) .... we (14) .... some skating. We (15) .... even play some tennis.

PRACTICE 8

How to play table tennis.

Here is an extract from a book about the game.

> **Important words**
> point (n.)
> score (n.&v.)
> match (n.)

'The bat is usually held with one finger along the back to keep it steady. The server stands about 3 feet behind the table. The ball is placed in the palm of the server's hand which must be flat. When serving the ball the player must hit it so that the ball falls first in his own court and then passes over the net to touch the opposite court. A player loses a point if he touches the table while playing a point. A game is for 21 points but if the score is 20-all then 2 consecutive points are needed to win. At the end of the game the players change ends. The best of five games is the usual way of deciding a match.'

(A) is teaching (B) how to play. Can you finish what he said to his pupil?

(a) .... by holding ....
(b) .... closer .... That's right.
(c) You must keep .... flat, like this. Right, you're ...., so let .... and hit it with the bat.
(d) You have to .... so that ....

(e) You aren't allowed .... If you do, ...
(f) If both players score 20 points ....
(g) OK, the score is 21–15, so ....
(h) The first player to win three games also ....

*Did you
know that . . .*

In the old days in Arcania, girls used to play on swings and compete in swinging matches. In this way they could see over their garden walls, as they weren't allowed to go outside.

'What's the score?'
'Fifteen young men and two grandfathers.'

11 SHE SEEMS TO BE THE BEST QUALIFIED

Important words

vacancy	interview (n. & v.)	skill
pregnant	qualified	experience
give up	graduate	machinery
post (n.)	qualification(s)	bonus
press (n.)	fluent	insist (on)
candidate	bankrupt	reference(s)
vacation	temporary	contract
part-time	permanent	colleague

A vacancy had arisen in Mr Kay's small office. His secretary, who was pregnant, was suddenly advised by her doctor to give up working. Mr Kay had to find a replacement quickly and he advertised her post in the press. He placed an advertisement in three newspapers. Several girls (and a few men) applied for the job. He looked through their applications and discussed them with his assistant, Mr Samuel, when he came back from his time off that afternoon. There were some good candidates, some not so good. One girl wrote that she had been trained as a cook but she didn't like working in hot kitchens. One man wanted to work as a salesman but thought that working as a secretary was the best way to start. One was a college student who wanted to earn some money to support herself in the university vacation. She only wanted to work part-time. But eventually Mr Kay made the appointment.

DIALOGUE A

Mr Samuel: Do you mind if I take a couple of hours off this afternoon?
Mr Kay: OK, but what for?
Mr Samuel: It's Jennie – my wife can't pick her up from school because she's got to wait in for the plumber.
Mr Kay: Trouble with the water?
Mr Samuel: It's those old iron pipes, they're leaking again. We reckon at least four of them need replacing.
Mr Kay: Right, see you later then.
Mr Samuel: Sure, I'll be back around four.

DIALOGUE B

Mr Kay: Twenty applications – that's not bad for one advert. I've made a shortlist of five, so we'd better call them for interview.
Mr Samuel: Will next Monday do?
Mr Kay: Monday, all right. I'll see this one first, Juanita Ling. She seems to be the best qualified.
Mr Samuel: Is she the graduate in business studies?
Mr Kay: Yes, and I hope she's good at typing as well.

DIALOGUE C

Mr Kay: Now, Miss Ling, about your qualifications. I see that you have fluent French as well as English and that you were working with your last company for four years. Tell me, why did you leave?
Candidate (A): Actually, I didn't leave. The company closed down.
Mr Kay: Closed down?
Candidate (A): Yes, it went bankrupt. So I was out of a job.

Mr Kay: I see. And have you been doing anything since?
Candidate (A): I had a couple of temporary jobs, but now I really need something permanent.

DIALOGUE D

Mr Kay: So tell me, why are you applying to work for my company?
Candidate (B): Well, I was trained in book-keeping and office practice and I'd like to use my secretarial skills.
Mr Kay: I see. And apart from typing what experience do you have with office machinery?
Candidate (B): I know how to use the telex machine and the photocopier.
Mr Kay: All right. Well, I'll think it over and we'll get in touch with you in a day or two. Thank you for coming.

DIALOGUE E

Mr Kay: Now let me tell you a few things about the job. You know the salary already. We pay a bonus twice a year and we give three weeks holiday a year. Office hours are nine to five thirty and we work a five-day week. Do you have any questions?
Candidate (C): Er, yes. Could I ask about sick leave?
Mr Kay: Sick leave? Well, I insist on a doctor's certificate if staff are away for longer than a couple of days.

DIALOGUE F

Mr Kay: Miss Ling is still my first choice, so could you give her a ring and I'll offer her the job. If she accepts I'll write to the others straight away so as not to keep them waiting.
Mr Samuel: Are you going to take up her references?
Mr Kay: No, there's no need to do that. I'm pretty sure we can trust her. If she accepts I'll write her a letter of appointment.

Notes

an advert: The short form of 'advertisement'.
bankrupt: Unable to pay debts due to lack of money.

a bonus: An extra payment.

take up her references: Write to her referees (who would write about her work, character, etc.).

curriculum vitae (see Practice 1): Latin for 'personal record'.

COMPREHENSION QUESTIONS

(a) What post did Mr Kay advertise and why?
(b) Was Mr Kay pleased with the number of applications?
(c) Why did the Samuels need a plumber?
(d) How many applicants was Mr Kay going to interview?
(e) Does Miss Ling have a degree?
(f) Why was she out of work?
(g) What particular skills was Mr Kay looking for in his applicants?
(h) How many hours a week does Mr Kay's office work?
(i) Was Mr Kay offering a full-time or a part-time job?

PRACTICE 1

Fill in the missing words in these advertisements.

> A (1) .... exists for the (2) .... of shorthand typist in an international company, (3) .... D 16000 a year. Good education required. Ring ....

> *Planet Industries Ltd*
> *Cement Manufacturing*
>
> Worldwide management and engineering opportunities
>
> Planet Industries is expanding its overseas activities and future (4) .... will be made in its branches in the Far East, Africa, the Middle East and Mexico. Well (5) .... and experienced (6) .... who are chosen will join as (7) .... staff and will receive training before their overseas posting. Some (8) .... posts (1-year contract) are also available in the Toronto office. Good education essential-(9) .... preferred. Apply with curriculum vitae to . . .

PRACTICE 2

You and your colleague (A) are interviewing candidates for a job. Practise this dialogue with him.

A: Right, we've seen all of them. Now, who's your first choice?
B: I think it's the second candidate, Miss Smith.
A: Why's that?
B: Well she ....

> seems to be the best qualified
> 's a graduate in business studies
> 's good at typing and shorthand
> 's had the most experience
> 's been trained as a secretary
> 's been trained in book-keeping
> knows how to use the telex

PRACTICE 3

Which phrases or sentences in the dialogues mean:

(a) I don't want to make them wait.
(b) I always want to see . . .
(c) It isn't necessary to . . .
(d) I had no work.
(e) I'll write after a short while.
(f) Able to type well.

PRACTICE 4

Can you complete these dialogues? Some of the above dialogues will help you.

(a) A: Apart .... selling books what else ....?
    B: She's good at languages and cooking. (See Dialogue B.)
(b) A: Thanks for phoning, but I always ....
    B: OK, I'll write an application letter and post it this evening. (See Dialogue E.)
(c) A: There's ...., I've already filled the post.

SHE SEEMS TO BE THE BEST QUALIFIED 111

      B: All right. I'll cancel the advert. (See Dialogue F.)
(d) *A*: Will you offer him the job?
      B: I'll .... I'll decide by tomorrow. (See Dialogue D.)
(e) *A*: What's your wife doing at home?
      B: She's waiting in .... miss the plumber when he calls. (See Dialogue F.)
(f) *A*: Shall I send the letters off now?
      B: Yes, please don't .... the candidates .... (See Dialogue F.)

PRACTICE 5

Some letters of application (from candidates who were unsuccessful). Complete the following short letter from each of the three unsuccessful candidates who are mentioned in the introduction to this Unit.

                                         (address and date)
Dear Sir,
In reply to your advertisement of August 15 in the Times of Arcania I should like to apply for the post of secretary in your office.

I should like to tell you that ....

I hope, therefore, that you will consider my application favourably.
Yours faithfully,
   (name)

FURTHER STUDY

Works Manager (Palmville City Council)
D 35000 to D 45000 per year.

The Works Manager is responsible for refuse, cleansing parks and gardens in the city of Palmville. There are seven hundred people employed in this group.
    We require a qualified person who has experience in managing a labour force. Local government experience not essential.
    We offer first-class benefits which include a good salary level, a thirty-five-hour working week, car allowance plus low-interest car purchase loan scheme, sickness benefits, a pension scheme and subsidised canteen.

Telegraph Assistant (Radio Desoto) D 25000–40000

Practical experience as a telex operator with a knowledge of controlling a message switching system. Full training will be given during the first six months. Hours of work: on an eight-hour shift basis averaging a total of forty hours per week, including nights and weekends. Some overtime may be worked.

Notes

refuse: Rubbish.
sickness benefits: Time off with pay during sickness.
a pension scheme: A system for providing a pension after retirement.
a subsidised canteen: The canteen, where staff can buy meals, is supported partly by company money.

> **Important words**
> pension
> employee
> shift (n.)
> overtime
> employ

PRACTICE 6

Some candidates have applied for the jobs advertised above. You have to explain the conditions of work to them.

(a) You'd be .... all over Palmville. We've got about 700 employees. We want someone with .... though .... isn't essential. We work a .... and apart from the salary, which you know about, there's ....

(b) During the first six months we .... Your hours of work would average .... and you might have to ....

PRACTICE 7

Two personnel officers of the Arcanian Civil Service are considering applications by candidates for a post in the Accounts Department. From their telephone conversation what details can you fill in on the form which is shown below for the candidate that they are discussing?

A: One more application came in this morning. A Mr John Hudson Park.
B: Is he Arcanian?
A: Yes, he was born in 1943 in Padang, he's married and a Catholic, got an address in Sando Apartments.
B: What about his education?
A: Oh, the usual. Primary school for six years till 1955, Middle School for three more years and high school for three years after that. Then he did a BA in history at Silvertown University. He left there in 1965.
B: Any military service?
A: Yes, straight after university. He was an officer in the air force in charge of pay and records. That took him to 1967. Then he was with the Metal Can Company for three years in their personnel department.
B: What's he doing now?
A: It says he's working for a correspondence college, Beckton Hall. He organises their courses and marks the students' papers.
B: Any references?
A: Yes, there's a Professor White and a Professor Bandari, both of Silvertown University.
B: Well, I'll think it over. If I decide to put him on the shortlist I'll let you know tomorrow.

ARCANIAN CIVIL SERVICE   Form P/7-21

Details of the candidate
1 Full name (CAPITAL LETTERS)

Surname.. Forenames.....................................

2 Date of Birth	Male/ Female*	Single/ Married*	Nationality	Religion
3 Home address				

4 Education record Educational institution / Location	Years attended From to	Degrees, diplomas and certificates obtained	Level (primary secondary post-sec. post-grad.)	Special fields of study

5 Employment record (short-term employment should be excluded)				
	Dates of service	Name and address of employer	Type of business and whether governmental or private	Brief description of duties including candidate's personal responsibility
Present post				
Previous post				
Previous post				

*Delete as appropriate

PRACTICE 8

> **Important words**
> foreman
> earn
> compulsory

A building site somewhere in Arcania. The foreman (the person in charge of a section of workers) is showing a party of foreign visitors round it. Naturally, they have a lot of questions, many of them about conditions of work. Some of the answers are given below. What do you think the questions were?

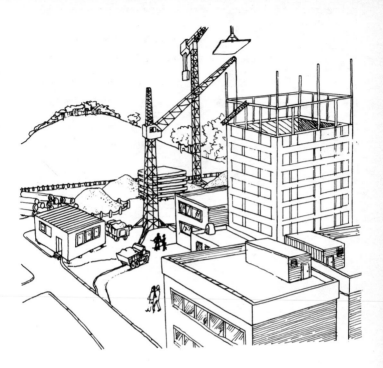

(a) About five hundred – some of them are permanent, some temporary. It depends on what we're building.
(b) Yes, they do an eight-hour shift, so the work goes on twenty-four hours a day.
(c) A skilled worker earns about six hundred dinars a week. Of course the unskilled earn a bit less.
(d) Yes, at the moment we've got several for electricians and plumbers. Quite a lot of them have gone to work abroad.
(e) They get one day off a week. And if they're on a contract basis they get three weeks a year.
(f) Yes, there's a low-cost medical insurance scheme. It's compulsory for all our employees.
(g) Yes, it's that building down there with the striped roof. Of

course, it's only a temporary one, but it saves them bringing their own food.
(h) Just over a year. I used to work as a crane-driver.

'And do you have any experience as a teacher?'
'No, but I've an unusual qualification for the job.'

The dialogues contained in the book have been recorded onto a cassette by native speakers of English. This will prove invaluable in helping you develop your pronunciation and listening comprehension skills.

The cassette can be ordered separately through your bookseller or, in case of difficulty, cash with order from Routledge Ltd. ITPS, Cheriton House, North Way, Andover, Hants SP10 5BE, price £9.99* including VAT, or from Routledge Inc., 29 West 35th Street, New York, NY 10001, USA, price $15.95*.

* *The publishers reserve the right to change prices without notice.*

CASSETTE ORDER

Please supply one/two/ . . . . . cassette(s) of

Coe, Colloquial English
ISBN 0-415-04567-3
Price £9.99* inc. VAT
   $15.95*

☐ I enclose payment with order.

☐ Please debit my Access/Mastercharge/Mastercard/Visa/American Express account number

Expiry date ....

Name ....

Address ....

....

Order from your bookseller or from . . .

ROUTLEDGE LTD
ITPS
Cheriton House
North Way
Andover
Hants
SP10 5BE
ENGLAND

ROUTLEDGE INC.
29 West 35th Street
New York
NY 10001
USA

12 YOU'RE SUPPOSED TO INSERT A TWENTY-CENT COIN

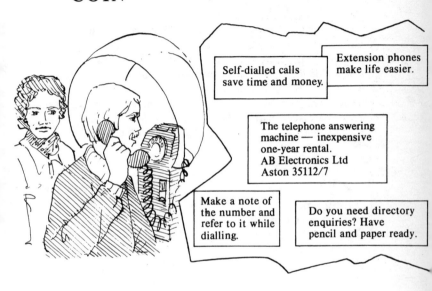

Self-dialled calls save time and money.

Extension phones make life easier.

The telephone answering machine — inexpensive one-year rental.
AB Electronics Ltd
Aston 35112/7

Make a note of the number and refer to it while dialling.

Do you need directory enquiries? Have pencil and paper ready.

Important words		
directory	cut off	engaged signal
extension	cargo	caller
put/get through	transfer	out of order
trunk call	fault	put right
dialling code	receiver	anniversary
automatic	reversed charges	greetings
operator	dialling tone	

Mr Taylor remembered that they had to confirm their return flight so he rang the Arcanian Airways office in Port Merlin. At first he got the wrong number, or, at least, the wrong extension, but in the end they put him through to the Reservations Section. A few days later he had to find a public phone and make a telephone call to the car-hire company because he had an accident with his car (luckily it wasn't too serious) and he wanted to report it. It wasn't very late, but for some reason there was no reply.

Mr Lee had some difficulty making a trunk call to his wife in England. He found the international dialling code in the telephone directory and tried to dial direct (there is automatic dialling from Arcania to Britain) but he wasn't able to get through. Eventually he got his home number through the operator, luckily still within the cheap-rate period. Once during the conversation he was cut off, but the operator reconnected him.

Mr Kay received a phone call from his young nephew who was touring in a distant part of the country. His nephew usually rings him when he is short of money or in some other kind of trouble, so Mr Kay wasn't very pleased to receive the call.

DIALOGUE A

Mr Taylor: Hello, is that Arcanian Airways?
Clerk: Yes, can I help you?
Mr Taylor: Yes, this is Jim Taylor and it's about our return journey to the UK – we're supposed to confirm our flight. Shall I give you the ticket numbers?
Clerk: Sorry, sir, you've got Cargo Section. You want Reservations.
Mr Taylor: Oh, sorry. Could you get me transferred?
Clerk: Yes, hold on a minute and I'll put you through.

DIALOGUE B

Mr Lee: Hello, international trunks?
Operator: Yes, can I help you?
Mr Lee: Yes, I'd like to make a call to Britain.
Operator: What number?
Mr Lee: It's Buckley 80233 and the code number is 8502.
Operator: Have you tried dialling direct?
Mr Lee: Yes, but I can't get through. There seems to be a fault on the line.
Operator: I see. What is your number?
Mr Lee: I'm at the Samyra Hotel, that's 048-7157, Room 217. My name's Lee. Robert Lee.

Operator: All right, would you replace the receiver and I'll ring you back.

DIALOGUE C

Mr Samuel: Mr Kay.
Mr Kay: Yes?
Mr Samuel: You're wanted on the phone.
Mr Kay: Who is it?
Mr Samuel: I don't know. It's the operator. Long-distance call, I think.
Mr Kay: OK . . . Hello.
Operator: Are you Mr Fergus Kay?
Mr Kay: Yes, speaking.
Operator: I've a personal call from a Mr Basil Moty. Will you accept reversed charges?
Mr Kay: Oh . . . all right, yes.

DIALOGUE D

Mrs Taylor: Do you know what? It's Freda's wedding anniversary the day after tomorrow.
Mr Taylor: Hey, you're right. Well, there's no point in sending a card so we'd better send a greetings telegram.
Mrs Taylor: I've half a mind to write as well. I'll get an air letter form when we stop at the post office. Anything else we need?
Mr Taylor: Maybe a few more forty cent stamps – oh, and some of those airmail labels.

DIALOGUE E

Mr Lee: Hello.
Operator: Mr Robert Lee?
Mr Lee: Yes, Lee speaking.
Operator: Your call to England. Would you hold the line a moment . . . Right, go ahead, caller.
Mr Lee: Hello, Vicki, is that you?
Mrs Lee: Bob. Hi, is everything OK?

Mr Lee: Yes, I'm fine. I tried to call you earlier but I couldn't get through.
Mrs Lee: Our phone was out of order – they've just put it right.

DIALOGUE F

Mrs Taylor: It says 'Lift the receiver and wait for the dialling tone'.
Mr Taylor: I've done that, *and* I've dialled the number.
Mrs Taylor: Then you're supposed to insert a twenty-cent coin when you hear the pay tone.
Mr Taylor: I seem to have got the engaged signal.
Policeman: Let me listen, sir . . . No, it's ringing but they're just not answering. Better try again later.

DIALOGUE G

Mr Lee: Damn . . . Hello, operator. Operator?
Operator: Yes, can I help you?
Mr Lee: Yes, we were cut off. Could you reconnect me, please?
Operator: Sorry, caller. One minute, I'll try to reconnect you.

Notes

self-dialled calls: Calls which you dial yourself and do not make through the operator.
directory enquiries: The system of finding out numbers through the operator.
cheap-rate period: The time of day when telephone calls are cheaper.
cargo section: The section responsible for dealing with unaccompanied baggage.
the receiver: The part of the telephone which you lift up.
a personal call: A phone call which is made to one person only. If he/she isn't there, no charge is made.
reversed charges: The person who receives the call pays for it.
there's no point in: It's useless to.
I've half a mind to: I'm thinking of (doing something).
the dialling tone: The note or signal that you hear before dialling.
Bob: The shortened form of 'Robert'.

COMPREHENSION QUESTIONS

(a) What extension did Mr Taylor need at Arcanian Airways?
(b) Why couldn't Mr Lee get through to his wife at first?
(c) Who paid for Basil Moty's phone call?
(d) What did the Taylors need to do at the post office?
(e) Why couldn't Mr Taylor contact the car-hire company?

PRACTICE 1

Fill in the missing words.

Why is this man angry?

First of all, there was no (1) .... so although he knew the number he couldn't find the (2) ...., so he had to ask the (3) .... Then, when he rang the number they gave him the wrong (4) .... and weren't able to (5) .... him, so he had to ring the number again. Then, when he (6).......... through the person he wanted was out. When he rang another number the line was constantly (7) .... although he tried it several times. When he rang the third number he heard it (8) .... for a long time but there was no (9) .... When he rang the fourth number the line simply went dead so he presumed the phone was (10) ....

PRACTICE 2

You have telephoned Kandodo Department Store. You wanted to speak to the furniture department about a sofa that you ordered. But the girl at the other end of the line told you that you had got the menswear department. You asked her to help you and she agreed. What did you both say?

PRACTICE 3

'Sorry, I'm supposed to . . .'

People asked you on different days to go out for a meal but you can't because (a) you have to wait in for a long-distance telephone call (b) you have to ring your nephew at 8.30 (c) you have to meet your wife at the bus station.

What do you say?

PRACTICE 4

What is another way of saying:

(a) Just wait a moment and I'll connect you.
(b) There's a telephone call for you.
(c) There's a call for you – will you pay for it?
(d) They aren't answering.
(e) It says you must put in a ten-cent coin.
(f) Would you put the phone back.
(g) I'll return your phone call in a few minutes.
(h) You can start speaking.
(i) Our phone isn't working.
(j) You've dialled wrongly.
(k) As we were talking the line went dead.

PRACTICE 5

'There's no point in . . .'

How will you use this phrase when you speak to someone in the following situations.

(a) Someone is looking for the dialling code but there's no automatic dialling in this area – you can't dial direct.
(b) Someone is holding the line but he's getting the engaged signal.
(c) Someone is putting a coin in but the phone is out of order.
(d) Someone is going to send a greetings telegram today but the anniversary is in three weeks' time.
(e) Someone wants to get an extension phone but his house is very small.

FURTHER STUDY

Emergency Services

Fire	Coastguard
Police	Lifeboat
Ambulance	Rescue

> **Important words**
> emergency
> rescue
> exchange (n.)
> authority
> heading

Call the operator
by dialling 999

Tell the operator the service you want.
Give your exchange and number or all-figure number.
Wait until the Emergency Authority answers.
Then give them the full address where help is needed and other necessary information.

It is worth remembering how to dial 999 in darkness or smoke.

Place two fingers in the holes directly to the left of the finger stop.
Remove the finger nearest stop.
With finger in '9' hole rotate dial to finger stop. Release finger and allow dial to return. Repeat operation twice more.

Calls to these services are free.

Notes

a coastguard: Someone who is employed to watch out for trouble along the coast.

a lifeboat: A boat for rescuing people.

an exchange: A centre (usually the name of a place) where telephone calls are switched from one number to another.

an authority: A body such as the police, fire service, etc.

Yellow Pages: In Britain telephone directories have information about goods and services on these pages.

> If you don't know *who* you want ...
>
> but you know *what* you want ...
>
> just look up the right heading in
>
> Yellow Pages

PRACTICE 6

(a) You ring the operator to report a fire on the top floor of the house opposite (it is late at night and the people are away). What did you say and what did you hear? Complete the conversation.

Caller: Hello, ...?
Operator: Yes ....?
Caller: ...., please.
Operator: What is ....?
Caller: It's 21736.
Operator: ....?
Caller: Oh, sorry, it's Welford.
Operator: Hold ...., I'll ....
Fireman: Newtown Fire Station.
Caller: Oh, hello, I'm at 24 Roman Avenue, Welford and .... Please hurry.
Fireman: OK, we'll be there as soon as possible.

(b) If the emergency number in your area is 900, what instructions would you give to someone for dialling in the dark?

(c) What reply would you give to the question:
'Where can I find out about making a trunk call?'
'Just ....'

PRACTICE 7

Mr Kay had been ill and was at home. A number of telegrams had arrived at his office and his assistant Mr Samuel rang him about them. Here are the telegrams.

> KAYCO, PALMVILLE
> FOR KAY FROM PALGON PRESS. YOUR LETTER 10 JULY.
> APPOINTMENTS REQUESTED ALLSAINTS COLLEGE AND FISHERIES
> INSTITUTE. WRITING.
> COLIN JEPSON

> KAYCO, PALMVILLE
> FOR KAY FROM BINTAN BOOKSHOP. ORDER FOR ARCANIAN
> GEOLOGICAL INSTITUTE DESPATCHED 30 JUNE WAYBILL
> 912-7783196.

> KAYCO, PALMVILLE
> ARRIVING 19 JULY FLIGHT LA 211. PLEASE MEET AIRPORT.
> OTTO FILER.

> KAYCO, PALMVILLE
> FOR FERGUS KAY FROM SHER SINGH AND SONS. REGRET TO INFORM
> YOU OUR CHAIRMAN DIED 15 JULY. FUNERAL 17 JULY AT RAMBAN.

> KAYCO, PALMVILLE
> FOR FERGUS KAY. PLEASE REQUEST GRIMLEY'S BANK STOP
> PAYMENT MY CHEQUE NUMBER 710882. EXPLAIN LATER. BEST
> WISHES.
> BASIL MOTY.

Notes

a waybill: A document that accompanies goods which are sent from one place to another.

What did Mr Samuel say about the telegrams?

'We got five telegrams in. There's one from Palgon Press asking us .... and they say .... There's one from Bintan Bookshop, they say .... There's one from Otto Filer, he wants .... There's another from Sher Singh, apparently .... Then there's your nephew, Basil, he's asking you .... and ....'

Some hints for Post Office users (from a leaflet issued by the Arcanian Ministry of Post and Communications)

Please pack parcels properly

> **Important words**
> fragile
> seal (v.)
> adhesive tape
> register (v.)

(Ask for a leaflet at the counter)

Air letter forms – may be sent to all countries. Enclosures are not permitted.

Greetings cards – may be sent overseas either by surface mail or airmail. In an unsealed envelope with not more than five words of greeting in addition to the printed text and signature, they may be sent at printed paper rates (see table page . . .).

Parcels – should be marked 'Parcel Post' and handed over the counter. For fragile articles the cover of the parcel must be clearly marked 'Fragile – with care'. Boxes should be sealed along the edges with adhesive tape and tied with string.

Postcode – please include your postcode and put your return address on the cover when writing to friends overseas.

Registration – all parcels intended for registration should be marked 'registered' in the bottom left-hand corner and handed to an officer of the post office and a receipt taken.

Notes

the postcode: Numbers and/or letters with numbers which are written as part of an address.
registration: Recording the despatch of valuable articles.

PRACTICE 8

'Could I ask you to ....'
'I'm sorry, but ....!'

You are a post office clerk. What will you say to a customer in the following situations?

(a) The customer is sending a parcel overseas and he says it contains a pair of drinking glasses. He has written the necessary address but nothing else.
(b) You see the customer putting some bank notes inside an air letter form.
(c) The customer has filled a birthday card with writing and then asks you for a stamp at the printed paper rate.
(d) The customer has prepared a registered letter and is walking towards the post box with it.

Sorry, Mr Smith is out.
Who shall I say called?

13 KEEP GARGLING WITH WARM SALT WATER

Important words

gargle	symptom	antibiotic
plaster	swallow	get on
cotton wool	infection	horrible
fever	vomit(ing)	insect
septic	painful	mosquito
prescription	swollen	malaria
surgery	injection	antiseptic
clinic	tablet	faint (adj.)
patient (n.)	powder	bandage
stitch (n.)	allergic	drug (n.)
treatment		

One morning John woke up with a fever – his temperature was around forty degrees and of course he didn't feel well. He didn't want his father to call a doctor but his father decided to call one. He rang the doctor from the hotel and after hearing what was wrong the doctor came to the hotel and gave John some medicine for a septic throat. He didn't need to write a prescription as he already had the medicine in his surgery. Twenty-four hours later John felt a lot better.

A couple of days after that Sarah had an accident on the beach. The family had driven to a beach away from their hotel. Sarah trod on a piece of glass and cut her foot. It started to bleed quite badly. There happened to be a clinic not far away so they took her there. The other patients in the waiting-room let her through to see the doctor. The doctor cleaned the wound and put a few stitches in it. Sarah felt a lot better after the treatment.

DIALOGUE A

Mr Taylor: How do you feel now?
John: I've still got a sore throat and I keep feeling hot and then cold.
Mr Taylor: I see . . . then I'll get the hotel to call a doctor.
John: No, really, I'll be OK, Dad.
Mr Taylor: You just stay in bed and take it easy.

DIALOGUE B

Doctor (on the telephone): What are his symptoms?
Mr Taylor: Well, he's got a slight fever and it hurts him to swallow. It's pretty obviously a throat infection. At first we just thought he had a cold.
Doctor: No vomiting?
Mr Taylor: No. He says his neck is painful – it's a bit swollen.
Doctor: All right, don't worry, I'll be there in about half an hour.

DIALOGUE C

Doctor: Now, would you lower your shorts?
John: What's that?
Doctor: Just an injection.
John: Will it hurt?
Doctor: Well, it won't hurt me! . . . There. Now, these packets. I want you to take one packet three times a day.
John: Er . . . What's in them?

Doctor: Two tablets, see? And some powder. Now, you mix the powder with water.
Mrs Taylor: It isn't penicillin, is it? We don't know if he's allergic to it.
Doctor: No, it's an antibiotic but it isn't penicillin. One more thing – I want you to keep gargling with warm salt water. But make sure it isn't sea water!

DIALOGUE D

Doctor: So, how are you getting on? Feeling any better?
John: I feel a lot better, thanks. But the powder tastes horrible.
Doctor: Ah, that's because it's doing you good.
Mrs Taylor: What are those spots on his face?
Mr Taylor: They're just insect bites, dear.
Doctor: Mosquitoes, eh? Well, at least ours don't cause malaria. Still, I should keep them covered up.

DIALOGUE E

Sarah: Mum, I've cut my foot.
Mrs Taylor: What? Show me.
Sarah: It was a bit of glass.
Mr Taylor: That looks quite deep.
Mrs Taylor: Where's the antiseptic?
Mr Taylor: I guess we didn't bring it. Nor the plasters.
Mrs Taylor: I wonder if there's a chemist around here?
Mr Taylor: There was a building with a green cross – we passed it just back down the road. A green cross means a clinic here, so let's try there.

DIALOGUE F

Mr Taylor: I wonder if you could help us. My daughter's cut her foot.
Doctor: Let me see . . . I think that needs a couple of stitches.
Mr Taylor: Really?
Doctor: It won't take a moment.
Sarah: I feel a bit faint.
Doctor: It's all right, you just lie down for a bit.

DIALOGUE G

Doctor: There, I've put a plaster on it. Everything's going to be all right. How does it feel?
Sarah: A bit stiff. It hurts to walk a bit.
Doctor: If you like I can put a bandage on it as well.
Mrs Taylor: Please don't bother. We'll make sure she doesn't get dirt in it.

Notes

first aid: Quick help for a medical problem.
a plaster: A sticky cover for a small wound.
a fever: If you have a fever your body temperature is much higher than normal. Some serious diseases are also called fevers, e.g. typhoid fever.
a prescription: A form filled in by a doctor, which you take to a chemist for medicine.
a surgery: A doctor's office.
a clinic: A small, local hospital, usually for outpatients (patients who come for treatment and then go home).
I keep feeling: This construction indicates a habitual or continuous action.
an antibiotic: A drug that kills harmful germs.
I should keep them . . .: This construction is often used for gentle advice and means 'I advise you to . . .'

COMPREHENSION QUESTIONS

(a) Why didn't John feel well?
(b) What were his symptoms?
(c) What treatment did he get?
(d) What else did the doctor recommend?
(e) When was the doctor joking with John?
(f) What had Mr Taylor forgotten when they went to the beach?
(g) Why was Sarah told to lie down?

PRACTICE 1

Fill in the missing words in this extract from a medical handbook.

How to recognise Blenkinsop's Disease.

About two days after (1) .... the (2) .... will have the following (3) .... He will keep feeling faint and will complain of a (4) .... throat. He may have some difficulty in keeping food down, so there may be some (5) .... About 24 hours later some spots resembling (6) .... bites will be seen on his face. The following (7) .... is recommended. You should keep him warm and give him an (8) .... once a day for three days of the drugs mentioned on page . . .. Use an (9) .... such as Sanox to bathe the spots on his face.

PRACTICE 2

Practise this dialogue with the patient.

Doctor: Well, ... ?
Patient: Oh, I'm a lot better, thanks.
Doctor: Good. So, keep .... ?

how are you today	taking those tablets
how do you feel today	gargling with that
how are you getting on	antiseptic
are you feeling any better	

PRACTICE 3

Practise this dialogue with the doctor.

Doctor: How's your leg today?
Patient: Better than yesterday, but ....
Doctor: OK, make sure you don't walk too far.

> it's still a bit painful
> my knee's still a bit swollen
> it still hurts to walk on it

PRACTICE 4

You have a sore throat and you go to the chemist for some antibiotic tablets. The chemist tells you that you need a doctor's prescription for them. He also asks you what your symptoms are and you describe them. What did you both say?

PRACTICE 5

Tone-changes on the most important words. Which were the important words in these recorded sentences?

(a) He says his neck is painful.
(b) Make sure it isn't sea water.
(c) It was a bit of glass.
(d) I wonder if you could help us.
(e) I think that needs a couple of stitches.
(f) I feel a bit faint.

PRACTICE 6

Treating a minor wound. Someone asks you 'What do I do?' What instructions will you give? Some words are given to help you.

cut off, plaster

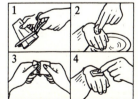

piece of cotton wool, bathe, antiseptic

the covering

press

FURTHER STUDY

Important words

sting (n.)   dentist   dose (n.)
liquid   ointment   headache
dilute   diarrhoea   period
solution

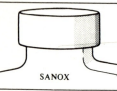

SANOX

Directions

Cuts, bites, stings and minor burns – Apply freely and cover with a dry surgical dressing.

Boils, spots, skin irritations and sunburn – Dab every few hours and allow to dry.

Colds, sore throats – At first signs gargle with the liquid diluted with about 5 parts of water and sip the last dessertspoonful of the solution.

Influenza – During epidemics use night and morning as for colds.

Mouthwash – Use daily diluted with about 5 parts of water after meals. For mouth ulcers apply undiluted three times daily and consult your dentist.

Other Sanox products:
  ointment
  throat pastilles.

Safe for internal and external use.

DIAMOL TABLETS

Stop Diarrhoea.

Dosage

Chew tablets and swallow with water.
Adults
4 tablets every 2 to 4 hours.
Children
(6–12 years) 2 tablets every 2 to 4 hours
(2–6 years) 1 tablet every 2 to 4 hours.

CAUTION

It is dangerous to exceed the stated dose.
Contents 52 tablets. Keep all medicines out of reach of children.

GARADIN

Headaches and other pains: 2 tablets when required.
Rheumatic pain: 2 tablets every 4 hours as required.
Colds and influenza: 2 tablets every 3–4 hours.

If symptoms persist consult your doctor.
Fast pain relief.

Headaches. Neuralgia. Colds. Rheumatic pain.
Period pains and pains following tooth extraction.

Notes

a sting: This is what you get from an insect, although for some insects, e.g. mosquitoes, we call it a 'bite'.

a surgical dressing: A piece of special germ-free cloth.

a boil: A septic spot.

irritation: Itching.

a dessertspoon: A medium-sized spoon.

a solution: A mixture of something with water.

influenza: The common name for this disease is 'flu'.

an epidemic: A widespread occurrence of a disease.

an ulcer: A small wound, usually on a wet part of the body.

an ointment: A medical cream.

dosage: The method of use.

a period: Menstruation.

PRACTICE 7

Someone is feeling ill. Practise this dialogue with him or her. Be sure to recommend the correct treatment!

A: You don't look too well.
B: No, I've ....
A: I should ....

> got a cold, I think
> got a slight headache
> been having diarrhoea
> got a boil on my neck

> put some Sanox on it
> gargle with Sanox
> take a couple of Garadin tablets
> have a dose of Diamol

PRACTICE 8

Getting relief and helping one another. Can you complete these conversations?

(a) *A*: This Sanox tastes horrible – it burns your throat.
   B: But didn't you ....? You're supposed to ....
   A: Oh, how stupid of me.
   B: And after you've gargled it's a good idea to ....
(b) *C*: They say there's going to be a flu ....
   D: Really?
   C: Yes, my doctor recommends ....
(c) *E*: What's wrong with him?
   F: It's diarrhoea – he's had it since yesterday morning.
   E: Give him these Diamol tablets – how old is he, by the way.
   F: Just seven.
   E: Well then, ...
   F: How should he take them?
   E: ....
(d) *G*: What are you taking those for – got a headache?
   H: What, these ....? No, I went to the dentist last Thursday and he pulled out a couple of teeth.
   G: That's quite a long time – I should ...., or your dentist again.
(e) *I*: What's the matter, does your mouth hurt?
   J: Yes, I've got a small ulcer on the inside of my lip.
   I: Are you putting anything on it?
   J: Yes, some of this Sanox in water.
   I: Actually, there's no need ....
      Have you seen ....?
   J: No, not yet.
   I: Why don't you ring him for an appointment?

PRACTICE 9

'I was sorry to hear your husband's ill.'

> **Important words**
> stretcher
> attack (n.)
> mild
> nurse

The woman on the left is telling her neighbour what happened to her husband the day before yesterday. What did she say? Some words are given to help you.

cutting the hedge

found him sitting, he said

the hospital

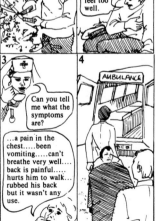

ambulance, on a stretcher

They said  They told me,

I asked them

visited this morning.

The nurse said

Perhaps her husband needs to join the Hash Physical Fitness Centre.

FAT

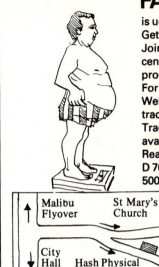

is ugly, unhealthy and mind-dulling.
Get serious about getting fit.
Join Palmville's physical activity
centre and start an individual fitness
programme.
For Men and Women.
Well-equipped exercise room, running
track, tennis, pool, sauna.
Track-suits, towels provided, parking
available, snack bar, massage room.
Reasonable rates: (men) entry fee
D 700, monthly fee D 80; (women) D
500, and D 60 monthly.

The Hash Physical
Fitness Centre
22 City Road
Palmville 9

14 THEY SHOULD'VE USED MORE WATERPROOF PAPER

Important words		
waterproof	van	screen (n.)
panel	clear (v.)	annoy
forwarding	workman	replacement
agent	load (v.)	fix (v.)
caterer	estimate (n.)	roll (n.)

The arrangements for Mr Lee's book exhibition were going ahead. When the books arrived Mr Lee and Mr Kay went down to the Publishers Association hall to arrange them on the tables. The boxes arrived on an open lorry and one of them was rather damp inside; probably it had been standing somewhere in the rain, although the forwarding agent usually stores the boxes under cover. Mr Lee was very annoyed as the same thing had happened in another country recently. He blamed the packers at his company.

The exhibition consisted not only of books: there were posters and photographs, some of which they fixed to the wall, and a film called 'Books for Sale' which they were going to show in a room next to the main exhibition hall (see the diagram on page 114). This room was rather small (about 13 metres by 6 but the big room alongside wasn't dark enough. They were going to arrange some of the books on folding tables covered with cloth and the others on panels that stood behind the tables. They had to fit the panels together first.

Mr Kay told Mr Lee that he had had to change the caterer for the exhibition reception. The new caterer, Mr Samy No, called to see them and said he would bring everything to the exhibition in his van by the middle of the afternoon.

DIALOGUE A

Mr Lee: Have they got the boxes out of Customs yet?
Mr Kay: Yes, they were cleared this morning. I've just had a phone call.
Mr Lee: So we can pick them up straight away.
Mr Kay: Yes, my assistant's going down this afternoon with a couple of workmen. They'll load them on to the lorry and take them straight to the hall.

DIALOGUE B

Mr Kay: About the reception for the exhibition – we've had to change the caterer.
Mr Lee: Oh? Why?
Mr Kay: Well, it seems his staff have just gone on strike. I guess they wanted higher wages and the boss won't pay.
Mr Lee: So who've we got now?
Mr Kay: A firm called Samy No. They're charging fifteen dinars a head, but that doesn't include waiters.
Mr Lee: And how many are we catering for?
Mr Kay: I reckon about a hundred and fifty. We sent out three hundred invitations but we always allow for a lot who don't reply and for others who just drop out. So a hundred and fifty's a rough estimate.

DIALOGUE C

Mr Kay: I'll get the workmen to open the boxes tomorrow morning.
Mr Lee: Where are you going to store the boxes?

Mr Kay: Oh, in the big room.
Mr Lee: You mean the room marked 'C'.
Mr Kay: Right.
Mr Lee: How about chairs for the film audience?
Mr Kay: We can get about thirty in, but the rest of the audience will have to stand. In any case they'll be coming in and out all the time. By the way, what about the screen?
Mr Lee: Ah, it's a special folding one.

DIALOGUE D

Mr No: Right sir, we'll provide the drinks and ten kinds of cocktail snacks.
Mr Kay: And how about the extras, for example, table cloths, flowers, etc.?
Mr No: Yes sir, they're included.
Mr Kay: And your people will get there by five o'clock so that everything's ready by six?
Mr No: No problem, sir, we'll be there by mid-afternoon.

DIALOGUE E

Mr Kay: We've opened the first box; look, some of these books are damp.
Mr Lee: They should've used more waterproof paper. I'm really annoyed with those packers – that's the second time in three months. What are we going to do about it? It's too late to order replacements.
Mr Kay: Actually, only the top layer's damp. The books underneath are all right.

DIALOGUE F

Mr Kay: That light needs fixing.
Mr Samuel: Which one?
Mr Kay: The one over there. It keeps going on and off.
Mr Samuel: Let's try changing the tube.
Mr Kay: OK, has anyone got a spare tube?

Mr Samuel: I daresay they've got one in the basement. I'll go and ask. We'll need a step ladder too.

Mr Kay: While you're there ask if they've got a hammer. These walls are so tough the pins won't go in.

DIALOGUE G

Mr Lee: I reckon we'll put six tables along each wall, there and there, and four along the back wall. Then we'll hold the reception down the middle.

Mr Kay: Right. How do you want those big medical books arranged?

Mr Lee: Better lay them flat along the front of the table.

Mr Kay: OK.

Mr Lee: Then we'll stand the medium-sized books in the middle and hang the smaller ones on the panels.

Mr Samuel: Mr Kay, we're running low on cloth. I'll just run down to the market and get a couple more rolls.

Notes

should've: Should have.

a forwarding agent: A company that arranges the transport of goods.

a caterer: Someone (usually a company) that arranges food and drink for a party and charges for this service.

a reception: A formal party, usually for a large number of people.

cleared: If you clear something through Customs you do the paperwork and then receive the goods.

the boss: Your boss is someone for whom you work.

drop out: An idiomatic phrase meaning 'fail to join some event or occasion'.

cocktail: This originally meant a special mixed drink. A cocktail snack is a small snack that you can pick up in your fingers.

fixing: 'To fix' is to repair quickly or arrange.

a step ladder:

I daresay: I expect.
running low on cloth: Haven't much cloth left.

COMPREHENSION QUESTIONS

(a) Why was Mr Lee annoyed when the boxes were opened?
(b) What did he blame the packers for not doing?
(c) What did the exhibition consist of?
(d) What was the area of the film room (Room B) in square metres?
(e) What did they need the cloth for?
(f) Why did they have to change the caterer?
(g) What was the reception going to cost (apart from the cost of waiters)?
(h) What kind of screen were they going to use for the film?
(i) Why did the light need fixing?
(j) Were they able to put the pins in the wall by hand?
(k) Why did Mr Samuel need to go to the market?

Arcanian Publishers Association Exhibition Area

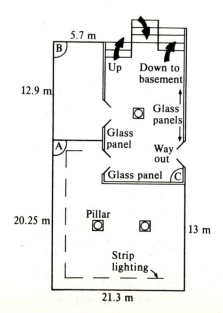

PRACTICE 1

Practise this dialogue with your colleague (A).

A: I'm afraid there's a slight problem. We're running low on glasses.
B: Oh dear, we should've ....

> ordered some more
> chosen a different caterer
> invited fewer guests

PRACTICE 2

And this dialogue too.

A: What's that?
B: It looks like a folding screen.
A: How do we put it up. Any idea?
B: I'm not sure exactly.
A: Better read the instructions so that ....

> we know what to do
> we know how to do it
> we don't go wrong
> it doesn't fall down

PRACTICE 3

.... should, shouldn't have ....

What will you say to your assistant if

(a) he has left some boxes full of books outside in the rain?
(b) he has bought four rolls of cloth instead of six?
(c) he hasn't used enough waterproof paper?
(d) he hasn't brought a hammer?
(e) he hasn't telephoned the forwarding agent?
(f) he has sent the van to your house – he hasn't sent it to the office?
(g) he hasn't told the workmen to come at six?
(h) he has left the office door unlocked?

PRACTICE 4

How can you reply to the following sentences?

(a) *A*: Plenty of lorries but no drivers! What's happened to them all?
    B: Apparently .... gone .... for ....
    (You've heard that they're refusing to work because they want more money.)
(b) *A*: Why are we starting so early?
    B: We've got to .... for ....
    (It's the rush hour and you wish to leave plenty of time.)
(c) *A*: I can't get these pins into the wall.
    B: Try ....
    (Maybe you could do it with a hammer.)
(d) *A*: Where are we going to hold the party?
    B: I ....
    (You expect you can have it in the room marked 'A'.)
(e) *A*: How much will the repair cost?
    B: I can give .... – about 500 dinars.
    (You can't say exactly.)

PRACTICE 5

You are going to put some furniture (it is for a public examination) into the big room marked 'C'.

Tables   Screens   Filing cabinets   Armchairs   Office chairs   Shelves   Cup-boards

---

Important words
symbol   adjust
filing cabinet   clockwise
plug in

(a) What do the following symbols (shapes) stand for?
   A triangle.
   A small rectangle.
   A half-moon.
   A rectangle containing parallel lines.
   A vertical rectangle.
   A rectangle containing two diagonal lines.
(b) In Room 'C', between the pillar and the opposite wall of Room 'A', you want to put four rows of small rectangular tables with office chairs, five sets in each row, facing the pillar. On the right-hand side facing the basement stairs you want to put one large cupboard and a filing cabinet (a small one) with an armchair between them parallel to the rows of tables and chairs. You want a screen between the armchair and the exit. Can you fill in the symbols?

PRACTICE 6

Fixing and operating things.

(a) The dimensions of each table for the exhibition were 240cm long by 105cm wide by 76cm high and each roll of cloth was 14 metres long by 60cm wide. There were 16 tables. How many rolls of cloth did Mr Samuel need to buy in order to cover each table completely down to the floor (better get your calculator!) Try to work it out in English.
(b) You want to buy a large fan for your office (see p. 148) and the shopkeeper has to explain how it works because the catalogue is in a foreign language. What did he tell you? (Later on you had the catalogue translated and the instructions were as printed below.)

'First of all, of course, you .... The knob at the bottom here is for .... – you turn it .... and .... If you want to .... you turn this knob at the back. If you want the fan to move from side to side you ...., otherwise you turn it to the right. Now, to choose the fan speed you .... and you switch it off by ....'

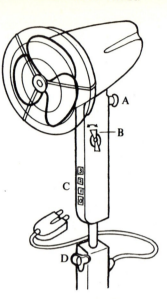

1. Plug fan in.
2. Adjust fan height with knob D (turn anti-clockwise to loosen, clockwise to tighten).
3. Adjust angle of fan head with knob A.
4. Knob B controls swivelling action. Left position on for swivel, right position for stationary.
5. Press buttons C (1–3) to control fan speed. To switch off press button O.

PRACTICE 7

Here is part of a publicity leaflet for an exhibition of garage equipment.

Please complete this registration form and hand it to reception at Garagequip '79 for free admission, catalogue and badge.

Name..
                                                                Block capitals please

Company ....
Address...
....
Position ....

Bring a party with you, there will be further registration forms available at Garagequip '79 reception. Monday–Friday 0930-1800 Organised by: The Society of Motor Manufacturers and Traders Ltd (Telephone 01-235-7000) for the Garage Equipment Association
24–28 September.

                                               GARAGE
                                                   EQUIP '79
                                               Olympia, London

(a) Mr A. M. Masoud, the general manager of Alliance Garages SA, PO Box 456, Monte Carlo, Monaco, intended to visit the exhibition. Fill in the form for him.

(b) Fill in the missing words.
At the exhibition Mr Masoud bought some electrical equipment which was sent to the (1) .... who sent it on to Monaco. After it had been (2) .... through Customs it was (3) .... into a (4) .... by some (5) .... and taken to his workshop. But when he (6) .... it together it didn't work. Mr Masoud was very (7) ....

'I pressed the button but I'm still here!'

15 THE DAMAGE CAN'T BE TOO SERIOUS

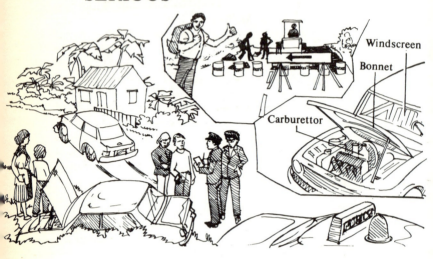

Important words

carburettor	mechanic	used (adj.)
bonnet	break down (v.)	attendant
windscreen	swerve	rucksack
scenery	doubtful	hitchhiker
set off	forecast (n.)	tyre
tarmac	motel	litter bin
detour	put up	breakdown (n.)
unmade road	view (n.)	block (v.)
flooding	reverse (v.)	witness (n.)
petrol station		

Mr Taylor and his family decided to make a trip to a small fishing village, famous for its scenery, about eighty miles west of Port Merlin, but it wasn't their lucky day. They set off early in clear weather and the scenery was very picturesque, but not long after they got off the motorway they found the road up. Some workmen were spraying tarmac on it. There was a long detour over a rough, unmade road which was made worse due to recent flooding. Mr Taylor was also getting some trouble with the car. When they stopped at a petrol station he asked if there was a mechanic who could check the carburettor. But the mechanic was off for lunch. Not long afterwards Mr Taylor had to stop again when the car broke down. While he was looking under the bonnet another car hit him behind, swerving across the road before it stopped on the right-hand side.

A passing police car stopped and Mr Taylor and the other driver reported the accident to the police. Mr Taylor also telephoned the car-hire company and told them what had happened. He requested them to supply another car – they were rather doubtful about this at first but it was in the terms of their contract and the manager said they would keep their promise.

DIALOGUE A

Mr Taylor: About our trip to Kolon – do you want to go tomorrow or would you rather put it off till Sunday?

Mrs Taylor: I don't mind, maybe tomorrow. What's the weather forecast, though?

Mr Taylor: Probably showers and sunny intervals. It always says that.

Mrs Taylor: Do you reckon it'll stay fine?

Mr Taylor: Very likely.

Mrs Taylor: Well let's risk it and go tomorrow.

Mr Taylor: There's a motel at Kolon under the same management as this one. Maybe they could put us up for the night.

Mrs Taylor: I think I'd rather come back.

Mr Taylor: OK, well, let's set off early, then.

DIALOGUE B

Mrs Taylor: Jim, there's a really good view over there.

Mr Taylor: Sorry, can't stop here, there's nowhere to park.

Sarah: What about there?

Mr Taylor: That's no use, that's a path to someone's farm. Hang on, there's a place on the left there . . . OK, I'll go a bit further and reverse into it. . . . . (starts to reverse) . . . keep a lookout on the left.

John: You're OK, Dad.

Mr Taylor: There. I wish they'd leave a bit more space at the side of the road.

Mrs Taylor: They seem to grow things right up to the edge.

Mr Taylor: And I'm still not used to this car – I can't see the back of it when I'm reversing.

DIALOGUE C

Mrs Taylor: What's that sign?

Mr Taylor: Does it mean 'detour' or 'one-way traffic'? I can't tell the difference.

Mrs Taylor: Ah yes, the road's up. It's a detour.

Mr Taylor: Over an unmade road!

Mrs Taylor: Maybe we'd better turn back.

Mr Taylor: I wonder how long it lasts.

Mrs Taylor: We could ask that chap over there.

Mr Taylor: What, that chap with the rucksack? He isn't a workman. I think he wants a lift. (to the hitchhiker) Sorry, we've no room!

DIALOGUE D

Mr Taylor: (to the petrol station attendant) Could you fill it up, please? I think it'll take about thirty litres.

Attendant: Right, sir. Premium?

Mr Taylor: Please. And could you check the oil and water.

Mrs Taylor: We'd better clean the windscreen too – it's filthy.

Attendant: Shall I do your battery and tyres as well?

Mr Taylor: Thanks, good idea.

Mrs Taylor: I'll find a litter bin and get rid of this rubbish.

Mr Taylor: By the way, is there a mechanic around? I'm getting some trouble with the carburettor.

Attendant: Sorry sir, he's off for lunch.

Mr Taylor: OK, never mind.

DIALOGUE E

Policeman: Can you tell me exactly what happened?
Mr Taylor: Yes, I parked the car and got out to look under the bonnet. I know I shouldn't have parked on a bend but I couldn't help it – I had a breakdown, something went wrong with the engine. Then the other car hit me behind. Anyway, he was travelling pretty fast.
Other driver: It wasn't my fault – I swerved but I couldn't avoid him.
Policeman: Can you still drive the car?
Mr Taylor: I've no idea. Let's have a look. (starts engine) Yes, it seems to go all right.
Policeman: (to other driver) Better move your car, it's blocking the road.

DIALOGUE F

Mr Taylor: (on the phone) There's some damage to the rear offside wing. I've got all the other driver's details and I've reported it to the police.
Clerk: I see, sir. And the car is still driveable? So the damage can't be too serious.
Mr Taylor: Yes, I can get the car back to you but of course I can't use it as it is. So could I ask about a replacement car?
Clerk: Well, it is rather short notice, sir.
Mr Taylor: But it's in your contract.
Clerk: That's right sir, we'll certainly do our best. You see we're a bit short of vehicles because it's the high season but don't worry, we won't let you down. Ah, here's the manager – I'll hand you over to him.

DIALOGUE G

Manager: Sorry to hear about your bad news, sir. Now, exactly where did the accident take place?
Mr Taylor: Let's see, it was between Gomi and Kolon, about ten miles along the turning off the Palmville motorway.

Manager: Any witnesses?
Mr Taylor: Only my family. The other driver was alone.
Manager: Was anyone injured?
Mr Taylor: My wife was bruised on the arm – she was the only one sitting in the car. Oh – one more point. The other driver's licence wasn't up to date. He should have renewed it six months ago.

Notes

a motorway: A fast major road with special rules.
they found the road up: The road was under repair.
a motel: A hotel specially built for motorists.
hang on: Wait a moment.
to reverse: To drive backwards.
used: Accustomed.
premium: The best grade.
a hitchhiker: Someone who waits by the side of the road for a lift.
I couldn't help it: I couldn't avoid doing it.
offside wing: The offside of a vehicle is the side nearest to other traffic. The nearside is nearest to the kerb (the edge of the pavement). The wing is the corner of the car over the wheel.
can't be too serious: Is obviously not too serious.
the high season: The busy season.

COMPREHENSION QUESTIONS

(a) Why did the Taylors have to make a detour?
(b) What did Mr Taylor find difficult about his car?
(c) Why did he stop on a bend?
(d) What was wrong with his car?
(e) How did the other driver try to avoid him?
(f) What did Mr Taylor do after the accident?
(g) How many witnesses were there?
(h) What happened to Mrs Taylor?
(i) Why was she hurt and not the others?

PRACTICE 1

Fill in the missing words.

THE DAMAGE CAN'T BE TOO SERIOUS

Mr Smith was driving along the (1) .... when a stone suddenly flew up and broke his (2) ...., causing him to (3) .... suddenly to the (4) .... side of the road. There were no garages for a long way, so when he came to the next (5) .... he made a (6) .... to look for one. He stopped at the first petrol (7) .... and asked the (8) .... to find the (9) ...., who was working somewhere at the back. While they were phoning the main supplier for a (10) .... Mr Smith removed the bits of broken glass and put them in a (11) ....

PRACTICE 2

You are planning to drive to a town several miles away. The weather forecast is bad and you telephone the Automobile Association for advice. Practise this dialogue with the clerk (A).

A: Can I help you?
B: Yes, I'd like some information on road conditions, please.
A: Are you a member of the AA, sir/madam?
B: I am. My number's Z04 632791.
A: Thank you. Which route, please?
B: The M 17, from Easton to Newtown.
A: Well sir/madam there .... and the forecast is bad again, so I shouldn't risk it.

> 's deep snow most of the way
> 's flooding for 3 miles past Oxley
> 's ice and fog on that route
> are several detours due to flooding

PRACTICE 3

Harry and Hilda, who are hitchhiking in the country, are walking along a path when they meet a large and rather angry-looking man. Practise this dialogue with them.

Harry: Er, does this path lead to the top of the hill?
Man: No it doesn't, and you aren't supposed to be here. This is
....
Harry: Oh, I'm sorry, we had no idea.
Hilda: Yes, we'll turn back. (later) I do wish they'd put up some notices in English.

> private land
> closed to the public
> a military area

PRACTICE 4

.... it can't be ....

Practise these short dialogues.

(a) *A*: How's your arm?
    B: It hurts a bit but I can still move it.
    A: Good, that means .... too serious.
(b) *A*: How's your battery?
    B: Well, the car started all right this morning.
    A: Ah, so .... too bad.
(c) *A*: Are we anywhere near Kolon yet?
    B: Well, I can see the sea, so .... far now.
(d) *A*: Do you recognise those houses?
    B: I don't. No, this isn't the way we came. .... the right direction.
    A: I guess we shouldn't have taken that left turn.

PRACTICE 5

What are they saying?

THE DAMAGE CAN'T BE TOO SERIOUS

PRACTICE 6

Tone-changes on the most important words. Which were the important words in these recorded sentences?

(a) Do you reckon it'll stay fine?
(b) Maybe they could put us up for the night.
(c) That chap with the rucksack?
(d) Can you still drive the car?
(e) Any witnesses?
(f) Was anyone injured?

FURTHER STUDY

Here is a map of the route from Kemi to Pula in the border areas of Arcania and Gwalia.

Important words
border
camp(ing) site

Notes
a filling station: A petrol station.
a service station: A garage where you can get your car serviced.

PRACTICE 7

You are a clerk in the tourist information office in Kemi and today several travellers ask you for advice about their journey along this route.

What do you tell them as you show them the route map?

(a) *Traveller (1)*: We'd like to see something of Kemi but we'd prefer to camp somewhere not too far away instead of staying in the city.
Clerk: OK, well .... (Mention how many kilometres the nearest convenient place is and whether it is north, south, east or west of Kemi.)

(b) *Traveller (2)*: Are there any motels along this route?
Clerk: .... (Mention the places and distances to them. It is also the high season, so what do you suggest?)

(c) *Traveller (3)*: I'm told petrol is quite a lot dearer in Arcania.
Clerk: That's right .... (Point out the last filling station before the border – but you aren't sure whether they sell premium, there's a shortage of petrol these days.)

(d) *Traveller (4)*: We're getting a bit of trouble with the van – it should be all right but if I have a breakdown where can I get help?
Clerk: As you can see, ... (Show him on the map, but ask him why he doesn't get it serviced at Kemi.)

(e) *Traveller (5)*: We're on our way to Pula but we want to make a detour to Balai village to see the old castle and we'd like to know whether to turn left at **Marisa** or **Rotama**.
Clerk: .... (You advise them to take a turning which is almost exactly half-way between – it's marked with a big sign board so they can't miss it – but warn them to expect difficult road conditions because there's been heavy rain in that area. Tell them you think it would be better to go straight on to Pula.)

PRACTICE 8

A road accident similar to Mr Taylor's. In this country they drive on the right. A driver is making a report to his insurance company: can you draw the accident diagram from his oral description?

'I was going north along Segonda Avenue, doing about 40, when the other car came straight out of a side turning (that's Alum Road) on my left, without stopping at the stop sign, and hit me on the rear offside wing. Then I continued for about 40 metres, then came to a halt and the other car stopped just behind me.'

THE DAMAGE CAN'T BE TOO SERIOUS 161

Onyx International Underwriters (Gwalia) Ltd
PO Box 545 Jupiter House Bala Road
Kemi Gwalia

Telephone
231-0742/6

Cable address
Onyxia Kemi
Gwalia

Automobile accident report

Automobile accident: ▭▷ = Your vehicle   ▓▷ = Other vehicle

Diagram

16 THERE MUST BE SOMEONE UNDER THAT FLOOR

GAS EXPLOSION AT LUSAC BUILDING

6 DEAD

6 persons were killed and 15 injured, some seriously in a gas explosion at Lusac build-

Important words		
explosion	sea front	stall (v.)
armband	bother (v.)	terrific
sightseer	blow up	

The Taylors were driving through Port Merlin when they heard a loud explosion. At first they thought it was the noise of a plane but before long they saw smoke rising a few blocks away and a little further on they came upon a crowd in the street and men with armbands directing the traffic. Mr Taylor asked one of them what had happened. He told him that there had been an explosion in a nearby building, though the cause was still unknown, and he told the Taylors to get out of the area as soon as possible. The way ahead was blocked and they were in a one-way street, so they tried taking a short cut down a side street and soon found themselves in a bad traffic jam. The car in front of them stopped and couldn't start again so Mr Taylor helped the driver to push it out of the way.

In the meantime two fire engines as well as ambulances and police arrived and the ambulance men began looking for victims among the debris. The police put up a barrier with a notice across the street leading to the building, which was badly damaged, and tried to stop sightseers from getting near. Two of the ambulance men heard noises while they were searching. It sounded like someone knocking so they took it in turns to clear away some bricks to get at the person under the floor beneath them. In the end they succeeded in rescuing him.

Some of those who had narrow escapes were interviewed by press reporters. Apparently the explosion had been caused by a leaking gas pipe and it looked as if the firm which had recently fitted the pipes was responsible for the accident.

DIALOGUE A

John: Hey, Dad, look over there – smoke.
Mrs Taylor: So it couldn't have been a plane. They must be demolishing some buildings.
Mr Taylor: I doubt whether they'd blow up buildings in the middle of the city. It must have been close to the sea front.
Sarah: There, look, where that crowd is, that building, it's on fire.
Mr Taylor: (to a man wearing an armband) Sorry to bother you but do you know what's happening?
Man: Don't know, there's been an explosion, and if I were you I'd get your car out of the way. We're trying to clear the road.
Mr Taylor: OK.
Mrs Taylor: What do you think it was. A bomb?
Mr Taylor: I doubt it. Probably gas or something.

DIALOGUE B

Mr Taylor: What a mess!
Mrs Taylor: It looks as if we're stuck.
Mr Taylor: Hey, you, in front, can't you move?
Mrs Taylor: Take it easy, Jim, he can't help it. His engine's stalled.
Mr Taylor: Right, I'll get out and help him to push . . . What's the matter? Want some help?
Driver: Thanks a lot.

Mr Taylor: You're welcome. By the way, can I get back to the sea front this way?

Driver: Sure, go straight on and you'll come to a big, grey wall. Then you can go either way.

DIALOGUE C

Ambulance man (1): Did you hear that?

Ambulance man (2): Yes, someone's knocking.

Ambulance man (1): He must be under the floor here.

Ambulance man (2): OK. See that beam? You lift the end and I'll start moving the bricks away. With any luck we can reach him before the fire spreads.

Ambulance man (1): Right.

Ambulance man (2): Can you manage?

Ambulance man (1): Yes, hang on, I'll need something for moving this lump of stone. An iron bar or something.

Ambulance man (2): Look out, that wall's moving.

Ambulance man (1): OK, I saw it.

DIALOGUE D

Ambulance man (1): Let's put him down there for the moment.

Policeman: What's wrong with him?

Ambulance man (2): He's got a broken leg as well as burns on the chest.

Policeman: Look, you've cut your hand.

Ambulance man (2): It doesn't matter. It's not deep.

Policeman: You won't leave him there, will you?

Ambulance man (1): Of course not, but I'm just going to ring the hospital.

DIALOGUE E

Policeman: Hey, you!

Reporter: Who, me?

Policeman: Yes, where do you think you're going? Can't you read?

Reporter: Sorry, I just wanted to take a few pictures. I'm from the 'Recorder'.

Policeman: Let's see your press card . . . All right, but don't get too near that wall. It's liable to fall down any minute.
Reporter: I can see that.

DIALOGUE F

Reporter: Mr Holden, can you describe what happened?
Mr Holden: Well, I was just going up the stairs, then round the corner there was this terrific bang. It must have knocked me out and I woke up lying at the bottom.
Reporter: Do you remember smelling any gas before the explosion?
Mr Holden: Well, there was rather an odd smell, a bit like new paint.
Reporter: And did you hear anyone walking around upstairs?
Mr Holden: I don't think so. It's hard to remember.
Reporter: Thank you, Mr Holden. I hope you're better soon.
Mr Holden: Thanks.

DIALOGUE G

Editor (1): That firm that fitted the pipes – they're being blamed for the accident.
Editor (2): I'm not surprised!
Editor (1): And another thing – their managing director's upset because he says we suggested it in our article last Friday. He's talking about legal action.
Editor (2): I don't like the sound of that.
Editor (1): Anyway, there could be trouble. I was going to spend the weekend out of town, but I've decided against it.

Notes

an armband: A band of cloth worn round the arm.
debris: Broken pieces from a building.
took it in turns: One did it, then the other (Note: 'Whose turn is it?' 'It's my turn.').
a narrow escape: A lucky escape, just in time.
if I were you: I advise you to . . .

to stall: To stop by accident (of an engine).
the sea front: The edge of the land, usually a road or path, running along by the sea.
a beam: A heavy length of wood.
legal action: If you take legal action against someone, you bring a charge against him in court.

COMPREHENSION QUESTIONS

(a) What were the men with armbands doing?
(b) Why did Mr Taylor drive down a side street?
(c) Why couldn't the driver in front of him move?
(d) What did Mr Taylor help him to do?
(e) Why did the police put up a barrier?
(f) What did the ambulance men take it in turns to do?
(g) What did they do this for?
(h) What was the reporter warned about?
(i) What had caused the explosion?
(j) Who was being blamed for the accident?
(k) Why did the editor intend to cancel his weekend out of town?

PRACTICE 1

Two guards, (A) and (B), are walking through a building. It is Sunday afternoon and the building should be empty. They hear a noise. What do they say to each other?

A: Did you hear that?
B: I did! It sounded like knocking.
A: There must be someone ....
B: He must have been here ....

| behind that door in that cupboard lying under one of those lorries | all night since Friday evening since the doors were locked |

PRACTICE 2

You are standing in a queue at the airport, watching a small group of men. Practise this dialogue with the passenger next to you (A).

A: Those men with armbands – what do you reckon they're doing?
B: They must be ....

> searching everyone
> checking people's hand luggage
> waiting for the President to arrive
> stopping people from going through the barrier

PRACTICE 3

It is just before midnight and you are talking to a friend in front of your house. Someone walks past you and unlocks the door of the house next door. Practise this dialogue with your friend (B).

A: That's odd?
B: Why?
A: Well, it couldn't have been my neighbour. He ....
B: Who do you think it was?
A: No idea.

> 's gone on holiday
> 's away for the weekend
> walks with a limp
> 's just died

PRACTICE 4

Find sentences or phrases in the dialogues which suggest that the speaker:

(a) Doesn't think that something could happen.
(b) Feels unsure about asking a stranger for information.
(c) Is giving strong advice to someone.

(d) Believes that they can't move.
(e) Asks someone to stay calm.
(f) Asks someone whether he is able to do something.
(g) Gives a sharp warning.
(h) Attracts someone's attention rudely.
(i) Feels certain that something happened to him.
(j) Hopes someone will get well quickly.
(k) Is worried by a piece of news.
(l) Has changed his plans.

PRACTICE 5

Complete these short dialogues.

(a) *A*: (on the phone) I can't hear you very well, can you speak a bit louder?
   B: Sorry, I ...., I've got a sore throat.
(b) *A*: Hey!
   B: What's the ....?
   A: Get out quickly. The house is on ....
(c) *A*: Sorry, there aren't any bandages.
   B: It ...., I'll use this piece of cloth instead.
(d) *A*: Right, where's the leak?
   B: Over there. Sorry about the mess, the room's being painted.
   A: It's OK, I can ....
(e) *A*: How is he?
   B: It .... he's been knocked out. But with .... I can fix the rope round his shoulders and pull him up.

PRACTICE 6

Dialogues A and F will help you.

(a) *A*: You remember that old church that used to stand by the bridge? Well, it's gone.
   B: Really? They ....
(b) *A*: What was that bang? Any idea?
   B: It .... a plane.
(c) *A*: What's wrong with him?
   B: He can't move his leg. He .... it.

(d) *A*: That lorry in front – what's happened to it?
   B: It suddenly stopped. Its engine ....
(e) *A*: I thought your managing director was coming.
   B: So did I, but he just telephoned to say he can't come.
   A: That's odd.
   B: Yes, he .... against it.

FURTHER STUDY

Heavy gas leakage kills 9 in Tokyo

Tokyo (UPI) – Heavy gas leakage from a defective pipe left 9 persons dead and at least 26 others hospitalised in central Fujieda of Shizuoka Province, south-west of Tokyo, authorities said Monday.

Police said a doctor's family of 5, and 4 members of a 7-member family died when gas escaped in heavy volume from the pipe which had a crack in it.

At least 26 persons were taken to a city hospital in Fujieda, some 160 kilometres (100 miles) south-west of Tokyo and three of them were listed in critical condition. The gas leakage began as early as Saturday night but the local gas company which received telephone calls from alarmed residents didn't bother to check the suspected pipe immediately, according to police officials.

Notes

UPI: These are the initials of a news agency.
defective: Out of order.
hospitalised: Sent to hospital.
critical: Very serious.
residents: People who live in a certain area are residents of that area.

PRACTICE 7

You (A) are an English-speaking resident of Fujieda and you are interviewed by a reporter of the UPI news agency. What do you tell him about the accident?

Reporter: First can you tell me how the gas leak occurred?
A: Well, apparently .... with the pipe and the gas just leaked out.
Reporter: And the number of victims?
A: As far as I know .... They say that three of them ....
Reporter: I understand the gas company is being blamed.
A: Well, no wonder! Some of us ....but .... until Monday morning.

PRACTICE 8

'Can you describe what happened?'

Mr Leon Hall is an Australian tourist. He had an unpleasant experience on the first night at his hotel in Palmville. The police were called to the hotel and he told them what must have happened.

(a) Can you retell his story, using the notes that the policeman made?

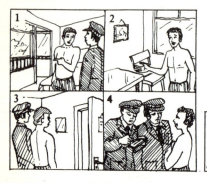

Important words
balcony
fire escape
properly
enquiries

Luggage may be placed here at owner's risk. Look after it, please.

'It happened while I was asleep . . .'

doesn't remember – hear anything – thief – climb on balcony – (?) fire escape* – door doesn't lock properly – suitcase on table – jacket and trousers on chair – taken out of door (found open) into corridor – doubt whether in room more than 10 seconds – report to manager 6.10 a.m. – missing as well as clothes: cash 450 dinars, traveller's cheques US $1000

The police made some more enquiries at the hotel, but the story had a happy ending. Mr Hall's case and everything in it, together with his clothes, was found in an empty room in the hotel. Only the money was still missing.

But the hotel manager told Mr Hall that since the hotel was responsible for the balcony door that didn't lock properly he was willing to refund the cash that he had lost. Mr Hall said that he was really very grateful. The manager also suggested he ring the bank to report the loss of his traveller's cheques.

(b) What exactly did the manager and Mr Hall say to each other?

PRACTICE 9

Fill in the missing words in this news item.

Due to the fact that the stairs and fire (1) .... were destroyed in the (2) .... the firemen had to lower victims from the (3) .... Police and helpers wearing (4) .... had to keep back (5) .... who were preventing rescue services from dealing with the situation (6) ....

Never mind – you can have your turn again.

17 IT'S TIME WE CUT THE TAPE

Mr Fergus Kay of F.H. Kay Ltd
and Mr R Lee of Dumas Books Ltd
request the pleasure of the company of

at the opening of an exhibition of
British books at the Arcanian
Publishers Association, 11 Museum
Street, Palmville, at 6.30 p.m. on
Thursday, August 8th 19...

R.S.V.P.
Tel. 171-3457

Important words		
engagement	introduce	see out
congratulate	responsible	joke (v.)
host	range (n.)	rude
retired	catch up (with)	mood
drunk	apology	greedy

Mr Kay had invited several VIPs to the opening of the book exhibition, among them Sir John Moulton, the British ambassador in Arcania. Sir John had recently arrived in Arcania and the President of the Arcanian Publishers Association, Mr Sety, had sent him some books on Arcanian history.

Sir John joined the other chief guests in cutting the tape, after which he made a short speech and looked round the exhibition. He didn't stay long as he had another engagement that evening, but he congratulated his hosts, Mr Kay and Mr Lee, on the exhibition and then left.

Mr Kay greeted an old colleague of his whom he hadn't seen for a long time. Miss Sorak, the librarian at Plato University, rang to say she couldn't come to the reception because her mother was ill. Towards the end of the reception Mr Lee noticed one of the guests, a retired army officer, who looked as if he was a bit drunk. He mentioned it to Mr Kay who decided to go over and speak to him.

DIALOGUE A

Sir John Moulton: Sorry I kept you waiting.
Mr Kay: That's all right, there's no hurry. By the way, could I introduce Mr Peter Sety, the President of the Arcanian Publishers Association.
Sir John Moulton: John Moulton. How do you do?
Mr Sety: How do you do?
Sir John Moulton: It was very good of you to send me those books about Arcania.
Mr Sety: Not at all. I hope you enjoy reading them. By the way, I'd like to introduce my wife. She's a writer.
Sir John Moulton: Very pleased to meet you. And what kind of things do you write?
Mrs Sety: Well, short stories mainly. Actually, at the moment I'm writing a travel book.
Sir John Moulton: Oh yes?
Mrs Sety: It's about walking through the Gwalian jungles. I'm very fond of walking.
Sir John Moulton: I'd like to read it sometime. By the way, have you met Alan Brown? He's the member of my staff responsible for books.

DIALOGUE B

Mr Kay: The chief guests are all here now, Sir John, so it's time we cut the tape.
Sir John Moulton: Right, I'm ready when you are.
Mr Sety: Sir John, would you stand in the middle of the line?
Sir John Moulton: Thank you, if you insist! I bet I get the blunt scissors again. Right, are you ready? One, two, three, go! (he cuts the tape). I'd like just to say a few words, ladies and gentlemen. May I say how pleased I am to see such an excellent range of

books here and I must congratulate our hosts on arranging the display so well. I feel sure that these books will help Arcanians to learn more about British science and culture and I'm certain that this exhibition will make British–Arcanian friendship even stronger. Thank you.

DIALOGUE C

Mr Danby: Mr Kay.

Mr Kay: Hello! Haven't seen you for ages.

Mr Danby: Actually I meant to ring you. We moved to a new office in June, then I was on holiday for a while at Mount Zebu.

Mr Kay: That's where we went last year. Beautiful, isn't it? Did you enjoy it?

Mr Danby: Oh yes, wonderful place.

Mr Kay: So what are you doing these days?

Mr Danby: Trying to catch up with my work, mainly, but it was very nice to get your invitation. Anyway, you must come over for a drink sometime.

Mr Kay: Thanks, I'd love to.

DIALOGUE D

Sir John Moulton: Well done, Mr Lee. Congratulations on your display.

Mr Lee: Thank you very much.

Sir John Moulton: I should think you'll get some good orders.

Mr Lee: I certainly hope so.

Sir John Moulton: Now, would you excuse me? I've got another engagement so I'll have to be going.

Mr Kay: Of course. Thank you for coming.

Sir John Moulton: Thank you for inviting me. Goodbye.

Mr Kay: I'll see you out, Sir John.

DIALOGUE E

Mr Samuel: Mr Kay, there's a telephone call for you.

Mr Kay: Thanks. (to Mr Danby) I'd better take it. Excuse me.

Mr Danby: Of course.

Mr Kay: (on the telephone) Kay speaking.

Miss Sorak: Hello, Mr Kay? I owe you an apology. I was coming to your reception this evening but I'm afraid I can't make it after all. My mother's been taken ill and I've got to go down to the hospital.
Mr Kay: Very sorry to hear it. I hope it's nothing serious.
Miss Sorak: Well, they aren't sure. They've got to do some tests.
Mr Kay: Well, thank you for letting me know. Let me know if there's anything I can do.
Miss Sorak: Thanks. Goodbye.
Mr Kay: Goodbye.

DIALOGUE F

Mr Took: Do you mind if I join you?
Mr Samuel: Please do.
Mr Took: I'm Alan Took. I work at St Jude's Training College.
Mr Samuel: How do you do? Fred Samuel. And what do you do at the College?
Mr Took: I'm in charge of the science department.
Mr Samuel: Have you been here long?
Mr Took: Just over a year. By the way, haven't I seen your picture in the paper recently?
Mr Samuel: Ah, that must have been the national tennis championships last week.
Mr Took: That's right – you won a cup.
Mr Samuel: Well, I guess I was lucky. How about you? Do you play?
Mr Took: I used to, but I'm out of practice these days. I must see about joining a club sometime.

DIALOGUE G

Mr Lee: That chap alone over there – who is he?
Mr Kay: Him? That's Colonel Marcus. He's retired, owns a bookshop.
Mr Lee: Well, I think he's drunk.
Mr Kay: What? You're joking.
Mr Lee: No, I'm serious. I was talking to him just now – he had a drink in each hand and he kept spilling it down his jacket. Most of

the time he was talking nonsense. And he's been pretty rude to the waiters.

Mr Kay: He certainly looks in a bad mood.

Mr Lee: Look at him now. I reckon he's going to fall over any minute.

Mr Kay: If he does it'll serve him right for being so greedy. OK. I'll have a word with him.

Notes

RSVP: These are the initials of a French phrase which means 'Please reply'.

It's time we cut: 'Cut' is past tense.

VIP: A very important person.

I can't make it: I can't get there.

been taken ill: Has become ill.

retired: Mr Kay means that Colonel Marcus has retired from the army.

it'll serve him right: It'll be his fault.

COMPREHENSION QUESTIONS

(a) How do you know that Sir John Moulton was late?
(b) What did he joke about at the tape-cutting?
(c) Why hadn't Mr Kay and Mr Danby met for some time?
(d) Did Mr Danby invite Mr Kay over for a particular day?
(e) Why couldn't Miss Sorak come to the party?
(f) Why did Mr Took recognise Mr Samuel?
(g) Had Mr Took been playing tennis recently?
(h) What was the matter with Colonel Marcus?
(i) What did he keep doing with his drink?
(j) Why did Mr Kay call him greedy?

PRACTICE 1

You are going to start a meeting. Practise this dialogue with your colleague (B).

A: It's time we ....
B: Right, I'm ready when you are.

> opened the meeting
> let the audience in
> called the first speaker
> gave out the papers

PRACTICE 2

What are the missing words?

(a) *A*: ………. to look after the children.
    B: Not at all. They were very good – I enjoyed having them.
(b) *A*: I'm afraid I can't pay you till Friday.
    B: That's all right, ……….
(c) *A*: Did you receive the flowers?
    B: Oh, sorry, ………. to thank you this morning but I forgot. Yes, they were beautiful.
(d) *A*: So he borrowed your bike without asking you?
    B: Yes.
    A: Well, I think he ……….
    B: Oh yes, he said he was sorry.
(e) *A*: ………………?
    B: No, only a couple of hours.
(f) *A*: There's something wrong with the typewriter.
    B: I know. I ………. getting it repaired.
(g) *A*: You've put bars on the windows.
    B: Yes, the local children ………. breaking in – I had to do something about it.

PRACTICE 3

What are they saying?

178 IT'S TIME WE CUT THE TAPE

PRACTICE 4

Complete these dialogues with the information given.

(a) *A*: It was ....
    B: Not .... enjoy the play. By ....
    ((B) has given (A) some free tickets for a play. (B) takes the opportunity to introduce her husband.)

(b) *A*: Sorry ....
    B: That's ....
    ((B) has been waiting for (A) at the bus station. (B) has checked the timetable and there is another bus soon.)

(c) *A*: So ....?
    B: Trying .... but .... Anyway, ...
    A: ....
    ((B) is at a party at (A)'s house. (A) wants to know what (B) is doing these days. (B), a painter, is trying to finish some painting. However, he invites (A) to come to dinner, without giving a date, and (A) thanks him.)

(d) *A*: ....! .... the race.
    B: ....
    A: I should ....
    B: .... so.
    ((B), who is (A)'s nephew, won the 1500 metres a few minutes ago. (A) believes that (B)'s team will win the cup and (B) expresses the same hope.)

(e) *A*: Would you ....? I've just .... so ....
    B: .... it. I hope .... Let me ....

A: Thanks very much and thank you ....
   (At a party (A) receives a telephone call to say that his brother has been taken ill. Therefore he has to leave right away. (B) says he is sorry, (A) thanks him and leaves.)

(f) *A*: ....?
   B: Of course.
   A: By ...., haven't we ....? I'm ...., I'm ....
   B: Ah yes, ...
   ((B) is having lunch in a crowded restaurant and (A) wants to sit at his table. (A), who is head of the music department at Northbank Secondary School, thinks he has met (B) before. He introduces himself – his name is John Zetta. (B) thinks they met at a violin competition last April.)

(g) *A*: You know those bananas that were in the cupboard? Well, Willy's eaten the whole lot.
   B: What? ....
   A: No, I'm .... And now ....
   B: Well, ...
   (Willy says he feels sick. (B) doesn't feel very sorry!)

PRACTICE 5

Sir John Moulton usually makes the same speech (as far as possible) when he opens an exhibition. Recently he made a short speech at an exhibition of British design and packaging at the Arcanian Design Centre.

He said he would speak briefly, that he was pleased to see such a range of exciting shapes of everything from the cups to television sets, that he congratulated the Arcanian Design Centre on arranging the display and that he felt sure the exhibition would help to develop trade between Britain and Arcania.

What were Sir John's words?

PRACTICE 6

Tone-changes: which were the most important words in these recorded sentences?

(a) I hope you enjoy reading them.

(b) I'd like to read it sometime.
(c) I meant to ring you.
(d) Did you enjoy it?
(e) What are you doing these days?
(f) Haven't I seen your picture in the paper recently?
(g) He kept spilling it down his jacket.
(h) I'll have a word with him.

PRACTICE 7

What happened at the party?

In the following dialogues we revise some of the phrases and sentences used in this book so far. Choose them from below each dialogue.

(a) You are on your way to a party but you can't find the house, partly because it is dark and raining and partly because you can't understand the map. You knock on the door of a house. Complete this dialogue with the owner (B).

  A: .... but .... number 56?
  B: Number 56. Yes, that's up the hill on the left-hand side.
  A: .... on the map?
  B: Let's have a look. Yes, it's somewhere about here, just after the bridge. It .... about ten minutes walk.
  A: Thanks very much. Er, ... it isn't near your house. Your house is 53, isn't it?
  B: Yes, but they gave the houses numbers when they built them. The newer houses are up the hill.

  must be; I wonder why; could you tell me
  the way to; would you mind showing me;
  I'm sorry to bother you but

(b) You are leaving a party but when you go to pick up your coat you can't find it. Complete this dialogue with your host (A).

  A: .... you didn't leave it in the other bedroom?
  B: No, ... in here. .... I look through that pile there?

A: No, ... I'll ring up the people who've left – maybe someone took it by mistake.
B: Well, ... anyone would take it on purpose: it's ten years old and the collar ....

I'm sure I left it; I suppose; I don't mind;
do you mind if; I doubt whether; if you like;
needs mending

(c) You have just arrived at a party and your host wants to know what you would like to eat and drink. Complete this dialogue with your host (A).

A: .... ? Some beer?
B: Thanks, but .... a soft drink. Maybe orange juice.
A: Sorry, ... we don't have any. Will Coca cola be all right?
B: Thanks, ... very well.
A: There's plenty of food over there. .... a plate, then you can .... put your bag over there?

what would you like to drink; I'm afraid;
that'll do; would you like to; I'll get
you; help yourself; I'd rather have

(d) It hasn't rained for 3 months and there's a water shortage. You aren't too worried because there's a spare tank in the basement of your house. Water can be pumped from here to the roof tank. But you have noticed that the roof tank hasn't filled up when the pump is on. Complete this dialogue with the plumber (B).

A: .... with the pump. Am I right?
B: Yes, ... there's no pressure. And the pump's .... it isn't ....
A: .... But how soon can you fit a new one. We're .... a party tomorrow. Could you do it today?
B: Sorry, I .... But I might be able to do it tomorrow morning, even though Sunday's my day off.
A: Ah, thanks, ...

it looks as if; I see; I daresay there's
something wrong; can't manage that; supposed
to be having; so old; worth repairing; that's
very kind of you

(e) You are having a meal with some friends at their house when
one of them is taken ill (he has gone to bed).
Complete this dialogue with his wife (A).

   A: He does feel hot.
   B: .... ice round his neck. That ought to bring his
   temperature down.
   A: I told him to be careful. He's been overworking recently and
   he .... these late nights.
   B: .... the doctor?
   A: Yes, maybe ....

isn't used to; you'd better; try putting;
would you like me to ring

(f) So you ring the doctor. Complete this telephone conversation
with the doctor's assistant (B).

   A: Hello, could you .... Doctor Bella, please.
   B: Doctor Bella's out .... Can I take a message?
   A: Well, what time is he expected back?
   B: Would you .... I'll look at his diary.
   A: No, please ...., it's rather urgent. I'll .... call
   another doctor.

have to; at the moment; hold the line a
minute; don't bother; put me through to

(g) You're having a very noisy party and about midnight there is a
knock at the door. You open it and see two policemen outside.
Complete this dialogue with one of the policemen (B).

   A: Hello, ...?
   B: Sorry sir, but there's a complaint from one of your
   neighbours about the noise.

A: Really? .... they didn't get in touch with us .... bothering you.
B: Yes, well maybe they .... but they rang us instead. ...., I ....
A: OK, I'll do that. .... a drink.
B: Thanks, but we .... to drink on duty.

how about; aren't allowed; what's the
matter; it's a pity; should've told you
first; anyway; instead of; suggest turning
that music down

(h) You have accidentally dipped your sleeve in a dish of hot soup at the table. Complete this dialogue with your hostess (B).

A: ...., have you got .... stains?
B: Oh, what a shame, you've stained your jacket. ...., I'll have a look in the cupboard. Let's see if I can find something. ...., try this. You spray it on – don't forget ....
A: Then you brush it off?
B: ...., there's a clothes brush by the mirror there.

that's right; to let it dry; here you are;
excuse me; anything for removing; just a
minute

(i) After the party you and your friend arrive at the bus stop to find that the last bus has gone. At that moment a private car stops alongside and the driver speaks to you in Arcanian. You don't speak Arcanian but your friend does. Complete this dialogue with your friend (B).

A: What does he say?
B: He's asking us if ....
A: That's lucky. OK, ... take us to the City Hall – no, on second thoughts .... he'll take us all the way to Shakespeare Road. But .... he's going to charge.
B: He says he can only take us as far as Liberty Square. That'll be ten dinars.

A: .... a bit more money?

ask him to; find out how much; that's no
use; how about offering him; let's ask
him if; we want a lift

(j) At a party in your friend's flat you have lost a small gold chain from around your neck. Complete this dialogue with your hostess (A) who has just heard about your problem.

A: ....your chain..........down the back of the sofa?
B: Yes – no luck.
A: .... in the bathroom. Have you tried there?
B: Yes, there's no sign of it.
A: Was it insured?
B: Yes, luckily it was.
A: Well, ... I .... the insurance company.
B: May I ring them from here?
A: Please do, I'll ....

how about looking; keep looking; have you
tried feeling; if I were you; should
contact; I was sorry to hear about

(k) You are walking away from the table with a large plate of food in one hand and a glass in the other, walking rather carefully. Someone you know (A) comes up to you. Complete this dialogue with him.

A: ....?
B: Yes, I'm all right. But there's .... so I'm going to the other room. ...., have you seen an ashtray anywhere?
A: Well, no. In fact .... they .... to smoke in the flat. They make the rule .... upset their son – he's allergic to cigarette smoke. But .... on the balcony you ....

can you manage; I was told; so as not to;
by the way; don't like you; if you sat;
could smoke; nowhere to sit

PRACTICE 8

Before Colonel Marcus got too drunk he told some stories.

Did'you hear the joke about . . .

the famous scientist who collected worms – he had a collection of worms from all over the world, but there was one worm he hadn't got. It was a famous black worm, very long and thin, and it was found only in a certain valley in Australia. So he went to Australia and found the valley and after searching for a week he dug up one fine, black worm. And he put it in a box and took it back to the hotel – but while he was at dinner the worm escaped. When he came back from dinner he searched everywhere in the room – under the furniture, in the bed – everywhere. Then he went into the bathroom and turned on the tap, and guess what came out?

18 IS EVERYONE IN FAVOUR?

Important words
consider	recommendation	restoration
monument	interrupt	preserve (v.)
arch	diagram	republic
council	alternative	original
tunnel	proposal	inscription
committee	funds	

In his spare time Mr Kay is a member of the Arcanian Independence Association. At present the Association is discussing a question which it considers very important. This is about the preservation of a monument known as Independence Arch which stands on a grassy island in the middle of a busy street near the centre of Palmville. Independence Arch was put up by the Arcanian Independence Movement to celebrate the end of British rule in Arcania. Although it is no longer the main national monument many Arcanians feel a sentimental attachment to the Arch, since it was put up on the exact spot where the declaration of independence was read.

Now, the Palmville City Council plans to build a new road to relieve some of the heavy traffic in the city centre. This is a big project, with a tunnel and a flyover (as shown in the picture above). If the flyover is built as planned it will pass almost exactly over the Arch. This will spoil its appearance and make it seem less important.

Mr Kay is the chairman of a committee of the Association which has been formed to discuss the future of Independence Arch. The committee will then make recommendations to the Palmville City Council. The other members of the committee are Dr Elias Chosuk, a professor of history at Plato University, Miss Ellen Potomak, a journalist and writer on archaeology, Mr Louis Chan, a lawyer, Sister Mary Dorada, headmistress of a girls' high school and Mr Peter Solomon, a tea merchant.

DIALOGUE A

Mr Kay: Well, we've all had time to study the Council's plan and . . .
Mr Chan: Sorry to interrupt, but have you got a spare copy of the diagram? Mine didn't come out very clearly.
Mr Kay: Certainly (he passes him a copy). So I'd like to ask for your views. As you know, we've got three alternatives. The first is to leave the Arch where it is. The second is to move it to another site. The third would be to demolish it and not rebuild it at all. I presume no one is in favour of the third proposal.
Sister Dorada: Certainly not.
Dr Chosuk: No.
Miss Potomak: Oh, no.

DIALOGUE B

Miss Potomak: Is there any chance of persuading the Council to change the direction of the road?
Mr Kay: At this late stage none at all, I'm afraid. In any case, as you see from the plan, the road passes naturally over the place where the Arch stands. No, there's no point in asking them to do that.
Dr Chosuk: Is there any guarantee that they will accept our recommendation?
Mr Kay: No, that isn't certain. But since they've asked for the

Association's views it seems likely that they'll pay attention to them.

Mr Solomon: Could I ask what the cost of moving the Arch is likely to be? I feel we ought to take that into account.

Miss Potomak: On the contrary, that's for the Council to decide. In my opinion we should recommend the best solution for the Arch itself.

Mr Chan: Yes, I support that. I feel it's up to the Council to find the necessary funds. Obviously the cheapest solution is to leave the Arch where it is. But that isn't necessarily the best solution from our point of view.

DIALOGUE C

Mr Kay: Let's begin by looking at the first proposal. As you can see, the road would pass three metres behind the Arch and two and a half metres above it, in other words more or less right over it.

Sister Dorada: Apart from the appearance of the Arch shouldn't we consider the danger to it from traffic? I mean all the fumes and the vibration.

Mr Kay: I don't think we need to worry too much about that, Sister. Don't forget that traffic already passes around the Arch and hasn't damaged it noticeably. I'm more worried in case the Council damages the Arch while removing it. We must also bear in mind that they might remove it to some unsuitable site. I'd like to point out that Pakot Island has been suggested and we know that often gets flooded.

DIALOGUE D

Mr Kay: We now come to the second proposal, which is to move the Arch to another site.

Miss Potomak: Sorry, I'm not clear how that would be done. I mean, can they do it without taking the Arch to pieces?

Dr Chosuk: Well, it might be possible to move it in one piece. But it's much more likely that they'd take it to pieces, numbering each stone. Then they put it together again in exactly the same order.

Mr Solomon: That's right. I believe that's what they did with one of the bridges in London. It was taken to pieces and put together again somewhere in America. I understand some millionaire bought it.

DIALOGUE E

Mr Chan: Could I raise a point about the upkeep of the Arch. I'm referring to the names carved on it. I had a look at them the other day and I noticed that some of them are getting a bit hard to read.

Dr Chosuk: I agree. I must say that in my view the City Council has rather neglected some of our old buildings. To my knowledge there are at least five buildings inside the City limits awaiting restoration.

Mr Kay: Well, as you know, this isn't the main point of our report to the Council. But if we intend the Arch to be preserved then it's a point worth making.

Sister Dorada: Yes, well, after all, those are the names of the founders of our republic.

DIALOGUE F

Mr Kay: To sum up, then, we're all agreed that the Arch should be moved to another site and that it should be a suitable site where members of our Association can hold their annual ceremony in a proper manner.

Dr Chosuk: Mr Chairman, could I make one additional recommendation?

Mr Kay: Yes, Dr Chosuk.

Dr Chosuk: I suggest that a metal or stone plate be laid on the site where the Arch now stands, stating that this was the original site.

Mr Kay: Yes, I think that's a good suggestion. Is everyone in favour?

Others: Yes. Hear, hear.

Mr Kay: Right, then. Dr Chosuk, perhaps you could suggest a suitable inscription for the plate.

Dr Chosuk: I'll do that, and I propose we add it to our report.

Notes

the City Council: The City Government.
didn't come out very clearly: Wasn't printed very clearly.

the upkeep: Preserving and repairing (the Arch).
restoration: Repairing in the original form.

COMPREHENSION QUESTIONS

(a) What Association does Mr Kay belong to?
(b) What is the importance of Independence Arch?
(c) What does the City Council plan to do?
(d) What is the Independence Association doing about the problem?
(e) To whom will the Association make recommendations?
(f) What were the alternative proposals for the Arch?
(g) If the Arch was moved, how would they move it?
(h) What was wrong with the names carved on the Arch?
(i) What was Dr Chosuk's suggestion?
(j) What was the result of the meeting?

PRACTICE 1

Fill in the missing words.

> The Arcanian Independence
> Association
> 12 Ulan Road
> South Hill
> Palmville

The Director of Public Works
  The City Hall
    Palmville

> 6 September 19—

Dear Sir,
At a meeting of a special (1) .... of the (2) .... on 5 September concerning the future of Independence Arch the following (3) .... was agreed upon.

Our (4) .... is that the (5) .... should be moved from its present site and rebuilt on a suitable new site. I hope very much that the (6) .... will (7) .... this plan favourably and will consult us about the site.

It is also recommended that a plate with a suitable (8) ....
should be laid on the (9) .... site of Independence Arch.

I look forward to hearing your views.

Yours faithfully,
  D. S. Menon
  President

FURTHER STUDY

Some of the uses of formal discussion in this Unit are:

(1) *Introducing ideas*
    Let's begin by looking at . . .
    I'd like to point out that . . .
    We now come to . . .
    Could I raise a point about . . .
    Could I make one additional recommendation.
    I suggest (that) . . .
    I propose (that) . . .

(2) *Breaking in*
    Sorry to interrupt, but . . .

(3) *Supporting*
    in favour of . . .
    I support that.
    That's right.
    That's a good suggestion.
    Hear, hear.

(4) *Asking for information*
    I'd like to ask for your views.
    Is there any chance of persuading . . .
    Is there any guarantee that . . .
    Could I ask . . .
    Sorry, I'm not clear . . .
    Is everyone in favour?

(5) *Disagreeing*
    Certainly not.

None at all, I'm afraid.
That isn't certain.
On the contrary . . .
I don't think we need to worry.

(6) *Linking*
At this (late) stage . . .
In any case . . .
As you know . . .
In other words . . .
More or less . . .
After all . . .

(7) *Stating personal opinions*
I feel . . .
In my opinion . . .
From our point of view . . .
In my view . . .
To my knowledge . . .

(8) *Stating facts and procedures*
We've all had time to study . . .
We've got three alternatives. The first is to . . .
There's no point in asking them.
It seems likely that . . .
That's for the Council to decide.
It's up to the Council to . . .
We must bear in mind that . . .
It might be possible to . . .
It's much more likely that . . .
I understand . . .
I'm referring to . . .
This isn't the main point.
It's a point worth making.
We're all agreed that . . .
To sum up, . . .

PRACTICE 2

Some matters for discussion. Complete the dialogues below with the information given. The numbers refer to the uses of language 1 to 8 above, in which suitable phrases can be found (you may have to alter them slightly).

(a) Gazonda Airlines have designed new uniforms for their air hostesses. But after wearing them for a week the air hostesses have decided that they don't like them. Their staff association chairman is having a meeting with the management to discuss the matter.

Staff chairman: You see, they (7) .... the uniform makes them look like railway porters and they dislike the peaked cap most of all.
Manager: Is (4) .... to accept the uniform with a different hat?
Staff chairman: Well, no, (5) ....
Manager: But at (6) .... I can't possibly change them. We've got thirty uniforms on order, ready next Tuesday.
Staff chairman: OK, but they're talking about a strike and we (8) .... the holiday season starts next week. And (6) .... all, we want them to be happy in their work.

(b) The Ibex English Language Teaching School is considering applications for teaching posts. Dr Jones, the Principal, is discussing them with two of his senior staff, Mr Davis and Mrs Gale.

Dr Jones: (4) .... on the application from Rufus L. Packer. He's an American citizen, born in Chicago 1954 and he's got a diploma in teaching English as a second language.

Mrs Gale: (7) .... all our teachers should be speakers of British English.
Mr Davis: (5) .... whether he's British or American. (7) .... if he's well qualified we should accept him and according to his references it (8) .... he'll be a good teacher.

(c) The Serbia football team, with a large number of officials, etc., is coming to play the Arcanian national team. Mr Turok, the President of the Arcanian Football Association, is discussing the arrangements with his colleagues.

Mr Turok: About their accommodation, are we all (3) .... the Scala?
Mr Poros: (4) .... they'll get single rooms?
Mr Turok: No, most of the rooms there are doubles, but we (8) .... most of them have asked for doubles.
Mr Long: Yes, and it's more (6) .... certain that the Scala will give us fifteen per cent discount.
Mr Poros: OK.
Mr Turok: Right, so (1) .... the arrangements for the match.
Mr Long: (2) .... have we got an up-to-date list of their names?

(d) Magnum, Ltd, a firm that makes metal furniture, has just been told of a large rent increase. Their directors must decide whether to agree to it or to move out of the city, where rents are lower.

Chairman: Well, (8) .... the landlord's letter and as I see it (8) .... – to move the office and workshop out or to move the workshop alone and find a smaller office somewhere in the city. I think we're (8) .... that we can't go on paying the rent of this place.
Director: (4) .... if other firms are being charged this increase?
Chairman: Yes, to (7) .... increases of 60 per cent are common this year.

(e) 'Lavo' is a washing powder made by the firm of Uniseal. Its sales have been falling and the directors of Uniseal are trying to decide what to do about it. They are near the end of their meeting.

Managing director: So, to (8) .... we're (8) .... the packet will stay the same size but we shall put five per cent more powder in it and colour the powder blue.

Director (A): (1) .... a point about the packet? I think we ought to make it light blue, like the powder. And (1) .... we print on it 'New Blue Lavo – the Packet that helps your Pocket.'

Managing Director: OK, that's (3) .... (4) ....

(f) The Citizens Association in the small seaside town of Marbella is worried about the unplanned wooden cafes and shops along its beach. The local Council, whose office is in the city thirty miles away, seems to be ignoring the problem. The Association has met to discuss the matter.

Mr Zafar: I'm (4) .... about the law. Are we allowed to put up signs to prevent people from building?

Mrs Robin: No, we can't do that. (8) .... take action.

Mr Zafar: But they're so slow!

Mr Salem: You know, very few of these new buildings have proper drains. (8) .... make the Council act over the danger to health.

Mrs Robin: Yes, it's (8) .... they'll take notice if we call it a threat to the tourist trade.

Mr Zafar: Right, (8) ....

(g) A British tourist in Arcania, Miss Jane Smith, has been accused of carrying drugs. The British Consul is talking to the governor of the prison where she is being kept.

Consul: I've spoken to Miss Smith and I (8) .... someone gave her the bag in which the drugs were found. She didn't know the drugs were in it.

Governor: On (5) ...., the bag had her initials on it. In (6) .... she must have known the drugs were there.

Consul: Well, but in (6) .... this was her first offence. Perhaps we can expect her early release?

Governor: I'm afraid (8) .... hoping for that. The police always prosecute in these cases.

PRACTICE 3

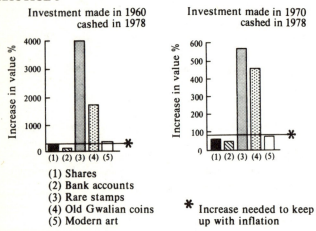

(1) Shares
(2) Bank accounts
(3) Rare stamps
(4) Old Gwalian coins
(5) Modern art

✱ Increase needed to keep up with inflation

Notes

an investment: You make an investment when you put money into something, hoping to get more money back later.

shares: Small parts of the value of a company are sold as shares to the public.

inflation: The decreasing value of money.

a dealer: Someone who buys and sells things as a business.

Mr Alpha, Mr Beta and Mr Gamma have been discussing how to invest their firm's new pension fund. Mr Gamma has been looking at the diagram above. A secretary took some notes of the meeting. Can you rewrite their conversation from the notes?

Alpha: requests views on investing pension fund. *Beta*: suggests putting in shares. *Gamma*: but over last 18 years shares only just kept up with inflation; over last 8 years haven't kept up with inflation. Would be losing money if all of it put into shares. Therefore proposes putting some into shares, buying rare stamps or old Gwalian coins with rest. *Alpha*: understands many people lose money buying and selling stamps. Any guarantee stamps would rise in value? *Gamma*: maybe possible to get advice from his brother (stamp dealer). *Beta*: if stamps, coins, pictures bought, would have to insure. *Alpha*: wonders if difficult to cash stamps, etc., at short notice. *Gamma*: shouldn't be problem provided they keep in touch with market prices.

'Any idea what it means?' 'Yes – it means they've got a lot more money than you or I.'

KEY TO PRACTICE EXERCISES

1

Comprehension questions

(a) Because it was once under British rule. (b) To arrange an exhibition for his company. (c) Change planes. (d) Yes. (e) 17.30. (f) At Palmville. (g) 17 days.

Practice 1

(1) via (2) exhibition (3) reservation (4) banker's card (5) travel agency (6) folder (7) receipt (8) insurance (9) valid (10) premium (11) account

Practice 3

Are our tickets ready, please?/ I'd like to pay by cheque./ What time must we be at the air terminal?

Practice 4

(a) The travelling time is nine and a half hours. (b) That sounds all right. (c) Fine. (d) Sorry? (e) Here you are. (f) It's valid for . . . (g) I see. (h) One more thing.

Practice 5

I'd like to book a flight to/ I believe there's a flight/ a flight on Tuesday at 13.55/ sounds/ does it take/ Two hours thirty-five minutes, sir.

Practice 6

holiday/ Hallyo coast/ express/ 10 minutes/ hydrofoil/ fare/ 9 dollars/ 1½ hours

Practice 7

Only (d) and (e) are correct.

Practice 8

I'd like to cancel/ baggage/ make a reservation/ ferry/ fare/ cabin

2

Comprehension questions

(a) Nine. (b) Because it was the rush-hour. (c) Because it was just inside the free allowance. (d) Twenty-five kilos. (e) No.

Practice 1

(1) Underground (railway) (2) counter (3) briefcase (4) overweight (5) allowance (6) departure lounge (7) announcing (8) sign board (9) passage (10) gate

Practice 3

(a) Excuse me, which way is the departure lounge? (b) Where do I go now? (c) Do I need to weigh my briefcase? (d) Have I got time to buy some coffee before the flight? (e) Have you booked my case through to London?

Practice 4

(a) Would you put your luggage on the machine, please? (b) May I see your baggage tag? (c) Could I have a seat in the non-smoking section? (d) Would you book my case through to Port Merlin?

Practice 5

Does my wife need to weigh/ lucky

Practice 6

(a) Over two. (b) The case is 28 inches long, 5 inches wide and 18 inches high. (c) If your baggage weighs more than the free baggage allowance you'll have to pay extra.

Practice 7

No, you're inside the free allowance.

Practice 8

(b) Change at Notting Hill Gate, take the District Line to Earls Court (or the Circle Line to Gloucester Road) and then the Piccadilly Line. (c) Change at Embankment, take the District or Circle Line to South Kensington, then the Piccadilly Line. (d) Change at Green Park, then take the Piccadilly line. (e) Change at Stockwell, take the Victoria Line to Victoria then the District or Circle Line to South Kensington, then the Piccadilly Line. (f) Change at Warren Street, take the Victoria Line to Victoria, then the District or Circle Line to South Kensington, then the Piccadilly Line.

Practice 9

Underground sign/ under 12 years of age/ fare/ destination/ route plan/ connects/ central/ under cover/ extra/ luggage/ in time/ trip/ airlines/ terminals/ platform

Practice 10

(a) Press the button, etc.
(b) Look for the, etc.

3

Comprehension questions

(a) 20.10 (b) Because another passenger wanted to sit in the same row as his family. (c) Because the passengers suddenly had to fasten their seat belts. (d) No. (e) No. (f) A pen.

Practice 1

(1) taken off (2) fasten (3) seat belts (4) change (5) take-off (6) delay (7) steward (8) sure

Practice 3

(a) We'll be taking off at . . . (b) We'll be opening the bar in a few minutes (c) We'll be giving out landing cards shortly (d) We'll be landing at Palmville at . . .

Practice 4

(a) There's something wrong with (b) Would you mind lending me your earphones?/ Not at all (c) Isn't this my seat? (d) Could I have a soft drink?

Practice 5

(a) In the overhead storage compartment. (b) While the aircraft is on the ground, during take-off and landing, in the aircraft toilets and in the non-smoking sections of the cabin. (c) Music, drawing books for children, games for children and adults and reading material. (d) Portable radio and TV sets. (e) Advice on the amount of duty-free goods allowed into each country. (f) They are supplied on board. (g) No.

Practice 6

(1) transit (2) transit (3) belongings (4) disembark (5) board (6) aircraft (7) security (8) prohibited

Practice 7

(a) Excuse me madam, do you mind not smoking before take-off?
(b) Sorry sir, pipe-smoking isn't allowed. (c) Excuse me madam, would you mind switching your radio off? (d) Please don't leave articles of value on board the aircraft madam.

Practice 8

Family name:	Green	Merton
Given names:	Harry	John
Nationality:	American	Australian
Address in Arcania:	American Embassy	Scala Hotel, Palmville
Purpose of visit:	Holiday	Business
Intended length of stay in Arcania:	2 weeks	2 months
Flight no./ Vessel:	AX 123	AX 123
Port of embarkation:	Copenhagen	Copenhagen
Port of disembarkation:	Palmville	Palmville

Practice 9

(a) all-night service/ Christmas Eve/ (b) downstairs/ invalids/ second class/ the engine room/ climb the stairs (c) deposit/ the barrier/ through the turnstile/ collect their belongings/ the gangway (d) hire a porter/ all the way/ taxi rank/ Lama Bay

4

Comprehension questions

(a) The health check, Immigration and Customs. (b) By public transport or private car. (c) Because there wasn't time. (d) Dinars. (e) The airline will deliver it.

Practice 1

(1) visa (2) arrival (3) immigration officer (4) currency (5) traveller's cheques (6) exchange bureau (7) rate of exchange (8) to

KEY TO PRACTICE EXERCISES 203

Practice 3

Customs officer: Is this a new camera?
Mr Taylor: No, it's just over a year old. I had a receipt for it but I've lost it.
Customs officer: All right. Have a pleasant stay.

Practice 4

Airline official: Can I help you?
Mr Merton: Yes. I've a problem. My briefcase is missing – it was booked on to this flight. Can you help me to find it?
Airline official: I see. Well, would you give me your ticket and baggage tag, sir. I'll check with the aircraft. Can you describe the briefcase?
Mr Merton: Yes, it's a black leather one and it's got my initials on it, JM.

Practice 5

(a) How long are you staying in Arcania? (b) Do I need/ country are you/ have/ visit/ apply/ an application form/ fill/ in/ your passport/ two photographs of passport size/ application/ 31 May (c) calling/ ashore/ you don't need a visa/ ashore (d) issue visas/ a stay exceeding six months/ apply to (e) No, you don't.

Practice 6

(1) applications (2) issued (3) applicants (4) missing (5) valid (6) applied for (7) dependants (8) call

Practice 7

(a) declare/ valuable/ duty (b) unaccompanied baggage/ be arriving/ submitted/ declaration/ what I can do/ very kind of you

Practice 8

change my dinars back into US dollars/ rate of exchange/ dinars to the dollar/ pink slip/ difficult

Practice 9

is it to the/ where do we catch it/ where do you want to/ would you put us off as near as possible to the tourist information office. How much is that?/ let us know/ stops

5

Comprehension questions

(a) It was shown on a notice. (b) Thirty-five dinars. (c) A cottage. (d) He borrowed his friend's roof rack. (e) There was a double bed instead of twin beds and no bath, only a shower. (f) No – he said they were rather full.

Practice 1

(1) reception (2) complain (3) matter (4) managed (5) flush (6) socket (7) air-conditioner (8) out of date (9) dated

Practice 3

(a) Ought we to tip him? (b) . . . is out of date. (c) I don't think we need to. (d) How far do we have to go? (e) No problem. (f) Why can't we take it? (g) It'll go on my lap. (h) Could you possibly change . . . (i) I'll just sort things out.

Practice 4

(a) notice, five (b) look, first (c) much (d) suitcase (e) lid (f) used (g) full

Practice 5

(a) could you/ change/ a double bed/ two single beds/ cottage/ problem/ get (b) sorted/ out/ moving

Practice 6

(a) Would you get him to drop me outside the National Bank? (b)

Would you get him to call at 11.00 pm? (c) Would you get him to pick me up at the airport at 4.30? (d) Would you get him to wait a couple of minutes while I go into a flower shop? (e) Would you get him to follow my route on a map that I'll give him? (f) Would you get him to change a 100 dinar note?

Practice 7

(a) By turning off all unnecessary lights. (b) By dialling 09. (c) By hanging a 'Do not disturb' notice on the door handle. (d) By hanging a 'Maid Service' notice on the door handle.

Practice 8

(a) occupied by one or two people/ 150 dinars/ no, breakfast is extra (b) it's about an hour's drive (c) two convention halls/ two banquet halls/ colour television (d) they're over 10 (e) to send a deposit/ one night's/ a hundred dinars/ accept credit cards

Practice 9

(a) Sorry sir/madam, there's a minimum charge of 15 dinars. (b) No tax is added for foreign guests, sir/madam. (c) There's a minimum two-day stay at weekends, sir/madam. (d) Check-out time is 12 noon, sir/madam.

6

Comprehension questions

(a) She thought they were too young. (b) The hotel doesn't hire out boats any more. (c) He was advised to drink boiled water. (d) There was no electricity. (e) Very soon.

Practice 1

(1) brochure (2) power cuts (3) electricity (4) off (5) boiled (6) flask (7) car-hire (8) hire (9) reception

Practice 2

would you ask him if I can hire a boat/ fifteen dinars an hour/ says it's only ten dinars an hour/ I won't pay more than ten/ him if the bay is safe.

Practice 3

what time he's planning to leave, how much food he's taking and whether he's bringing any ice/ but would you ask him to

Practice 4

He wants to know why there's no water; why the bank is closed; why there's no swimming; why dogs aren't allowed.

Practice 5

used to work/ used to live/ used to have/ used to be/ used to be

Practice 6

(a) Hire a boat?! (b) the hotel didn't hire out boats any more (c) to drink boiled water only (d) there was a power cut

Comprehension questions

Seychelles
(a) November, December and January. (b) 26.8. (c) From November to April. (d) No. (e) Because it isn't the local custom.
Alaska
(f) Clear, dry and cold. (g) No, not very much. (h) A heavy wool or fur coat, gloves, walking shoes and warm socks. (i) No. (j) A jacket and tie.

Practice 7

(1) seasons (2) humidity (3) rainfall (4) raincoat (5) lightweight (6) casual (7) wear (8) observe (9) custom

Practice 8

are you from Britain/ pleased to help you/ all the details/ of car do you want/ short of Datsuns/ and we have special low rates

7

Comprehension questions

(a) Maki. (b) By adding water. (c) Well done. (d) Prawn curry. (e) It makes her ill. (f) Black, with one spoonful of sugar.

Practice 2

(a) white (b) sweet (c) rare (d) hot (e) strong

Practice 3

(a) on me (b) my guest (c) I'm afraid/ there's a table free/ I'm afraid (d) pretty (e) actually/ would you like (f) I'm afraid/ could we have the bill/ a hurry/ separate bills

Practice 4

(a) bottles (b) that (c) ourselves (d) finish, Arcania (e) like (f) me (g) guest (h) one, do

Practice 5

Elysée/ worth/ rather not/ make/ ill/ to the Coffee Shop

Practice 6

(1) superb (2) atmosphere (3) décor (4) delicious (5) hospitality

Practice 7

(a) Prepare a special dessert. (b) Please help yourselves. (c) What's this dish made from? (d) How do you like your steak? (e) rather have plain boiled rice (f) Sorry, I can't eat shellfish. It makes me ill. (g) be back (h) it's home-made (i) through the doors/ turn right down the stairs/ the basement

8

Comprehension questions

(a) Yes, except where there are traffic jams. (b) He drove the wrong way down a one-way street. (c) Plato University bought books from his company. (d) No. (e) In a side street. (f) Twenty dinars. (g) She thinks they're boring. (h) Yes. (i) At the Publishers Association.

Practice 1

(1) excursion (2) fined (3) offences (4) Museum (5) speed limit (6) fine (7) traffic lights (8) driving licence

Practice 3

(a) turning right (b) parking in a 'no parking' area (c) driving his lorry where it wasn't allowed (d) keeping in lane (e) overtaking where it wasn't allowed

Practice 4

(a) Go down Hallim Avenue, take the fifth turning on your right, then go on for about 2 kilometres and you'll see it on your left on the corner of Jalan Road. (b) Go down Hallim Avenue, take the first turning right and it's about 1½ kilometres further on your right, on the corner of Jacaranda Street. (c) Go down Hallim Avenue for about 3½ kilometres, turn left at Gorsek Road and you'll see it on your right on the corner of Jeltan Quay. (d) Go down Halza Road and then keep straight on along Jeltan Quay for about 5 kilometres and you'll see it on your left. (e) Go along Hallim Avenue, take the first turning right, keep straight on, then turn left into Cortez Road – you'll see the Gardens on your left about a kilometre down the road. (f) Go along Cliff Road for about 3 kilometres and take the small turning on your right just before you come into Rose Street. You'll see the University in front of you.

Practice 5

(a) better/ lane/ going over the flyover/ left turn/ sign (b) pick/ no left turn/ pedestrian crossing/ won't be (c) first turning right/ U-turn/ turning before the bridge (d) we can turn/ U-turn/ underpass (e) no parking/ call at/ salaries/ side street

Practice 6

What happens if:
(a) sedans and taxis enter the city with less than four riders or without an entrance ticket? (b) they have less than four riders but have a ticket? (c) cars occupied by foreign diplomats enter without a ticket? (d) the police see vehicles breaking the law? (e) drivers don't want to come into the central zone by car? (f) drivers want to drive through the city without passing through the downtown areas?

Practice 7

(a) No, it belongs to my friend. He won't be long – he's just gone to the bank. (b) In this country they drive on the right but he has a right-hand drive car and wants to overtake a big vehicle.

Practice 8

(a) It says 'no pedestrians'. (b) It says 'no bicycles'. (c) It says 'no U-turns'. (d) It says you can't go straight on. (e) No, it's two-way traffic now. (f) It says there's a slippery road ahead.

Practice 9

a drinks party at home/ Thursday August 8/ hope you can/ busy/ an appointment/ Publishers Association/ the opening of a book exhibition/ like to come a bit

9

Comprehension questions

(a) He liked the colour but wasn't sure about the style. (b) They needed to be about half an inch longer. (c) How to take the candle holders to pieces. (d) She thought she looked awful in green. (e) Four.

Practice 1

(1) style (2) polyester (3) sizes (4) pair (5) slides (6) prints (7) department (8) discount (9) design (10) patterns (11) shaped (12) afford

Practice 2

(a) on second thoughts (b) we're out of stock (c) can I interest you in . . . (d) what are they for (e) could you give us some discount (f) I'm just looking

Practice 5

(a) We can give you 10 per cent discount on these madam – they're in the sale. (b) OK, but the sleeves need to be about an inch shorter and could you make the collar fit a bit more loosely?

Practice 6

(a) free trial without obligation (b) direct from the manufacturer (c) satisfaction guaranteed (d) free demonstration (e) money refund if not satisfied (f) cash paid (g) order now to avoid disappointment (h) a price to suit everyone's pocket

Practice 7

I took it to Kashgai Brothers and asked them to value it – I wanted to sell it for cash. Mr Kashgai said it was a little worn but that he'd give me a fair price. Then he suggested taking it in part exchange for another carpet. My wife thinks it goes well with the new flat.

Practice 8

(a) they aren't obliged to give you your money back if you simply decide you don't like the goods/ to change it (b) you don't have to pay for them (c) buy it on hire-purchase (d) under warranty/ return it/ manufacturer/ repair it or replace it/ defect/ free of charge/ the postage

Practice 9

sofa/ defects/ spring came through the seat/ worn/ had/ repaired

10

Comprehension questions

(a) She saw a notice about it. (b) She joined in. (c) No. (d) Twice. (e) No – they have riders. (f) No. (g) The dancer told her. (h) Not very. (i) They'll be leaving before that.

Practice 1

(1) festival (2) procession (3) spectators (4) handicraft (5) pottery (6) traditional (7) folk (8) concert (9) orchestra (10) programme (11) show (12) display (13) dress (14) interval

Practice 3

(a) that's a good idea (b) on the way in (c) what a pity (d) hold on to/ let it go (e) like to very much (f) well done (g) what do I do now (h) not bad at all (i) was bad luck (j) if you stayed on a few extra days/ they celebrate

Practice 4

(a) very likely (b) that's well worth seeing (c) we can't manage that (d) this is a waste of time (e) like this? (f) there's no sign of them (g) what a pity

Practice 5

only/ straight/ straight

Practice 6

(a) puppet (b) concert (c) now (d) lantern (e) flight

212 KEY TO PRACTICE EXERCISES

Practice 7

(1) went (2) could see (3) about going (4) would (5) would it cost (6) went (7) went (8) would cost (9) had (10) would cost (11) better (12) wouldn't cost (13) went there (14) could see (15) might

Practice 8

(a) keep the bat steady/ one finger along the back (b) Stand/ to the table (c) the palm of your hand/ serving/ go of the ball (d) hit the ball/ it falls first in your own court and then passes over the net to touch the opposite court (e) to touch the table while you're playing a point/ you lose the point (f) then two consecutive points are needed to win (g) we change ends (h) wins the match

11

Comprehension questions

(a) His secretary's post – his secretary was pregnant and the doctor had advised her to give up working. (b) Yes. (c) Some of his water pipes needed replacing. (d) 5. (e) Yes. (f) Her firm had gone bankrupt. (g) They had to be good at secretarial work, shorthand and typing, have good English and know how to use office machinery. (h) 42½. (i) A full-time job.

Practice 1

(1) vacancy (2) post (3) salary (4) appointments (5) trained (6) candidates (7) permanent (8) temporary (9) graduates

Practice 3

(a) so as not to keep them waiting (b) I insist on (c) there's no need (d) I was out of a job (e) we'll get in touch with you in a day or two (f) good at typing

Practice 4

(a) from/ is she good at (b) insist on a written application (c) no need to advertise (d) think it over (e) so as not to (f) keep/ waiting

KEY TO PRACTICE EXERCISES 213

Practice 5

(a) I have been trained as a cook but I don't like working in hot kitchens. (b) I should like to work as a salesman but I think that working as a secretary is the best way to start. (c) I am a college student and should like to earn some money to support myself in the university vacation.

Practice 6

(a) responsible for refuse and cleansing parks and gardens/ experience in managing a labour force/ local government experience/ thirty-five-hour week/ a car allowance, a low-interest car purchase loan scheme, sickness benefits, a pension scheme and a subsidised canteen (b) give you full training/ forty per week, including nights and weekends/ work some overtime

Practice 7

ARCANIAN CIVIL SERVICE   Form P/7-21

Details of the Candidate
1 Full name (CAPITAL LETTERS)
  Surname..PARK.....................Forenames...JOHN HUDSON.........

2 Date of Birth 1943	Male/ ~~Female*~~	~~Single/~~ Married*	Nationality Arcanian	Religion Catholic

3 Home address Sando Apartments

4 Education record

Educational institution	Location	Years attended From to	Degrees, diplomas and certificates obtained	Level (primary secondary post-sec. post-grad.)	Special fields of study
		1949–55		primary	
Middle School		1955–58		secondary	
High School		1958–61		secondary	
University	Silvertown	1961–65	BA	post-secondary	History

5 Employment Record (short-term employment should be excluded)

	Dates of service	Name and address of employer	Type of business and whether governmental or private	Brief description of duties including candidate's personal responsibility
Present post	1970–	Beckton Hall Correspondence College	Educational Private	Organising courses Marking students' papers
Previous post	1967–70	Metal Can Company	Private	Personnel Department
Previous post	1965–67	Airforce	Governmental	In charge of pay and records

*Delete as appropriate

Practice 8

(a) How many workers do you employ? (b) Do they work on a shift basis? (c) How much does a worker earn? (d) Do you have many vacancies at the moment? (e) How much holiday do your employees get? (f) Are there any sickness benefits for your employees? (g) Do your employees have a canteen? (h) How long have you been working as a foreman?

12

Comprehension questions

(a) Reservations. (b) Mrs Lee's phone was out of order. (c) Mr Kay. (d) Get an air letter, some stamps and some airmail labels. (e) He couldn't get through.

Practice 1

(1) directory (2) dialling code (3) operator (4) extension (5) transfer (6) got (7) engaged (8) ringing (9) reply (10) out of order

KEY TO PRACTICE EXERCISES 215

Practice 2

'Hello, is that Kandodo Department Store?'
'Yes, can I help you?'
'Yes, I'm .... and it's about the sofa that I ordered.'
'Sorry sir/madam, you've got the menswear department. You want the furniture department.'
'Oh, sorry. Could you get me transferred?'
'Yes, hold on a minute and I'll put you through.'

Practice 3

(a) Sorry, I'm supposed to wait in for a long-distance phone call. (b) Sorry, I'm supposed to ring my nephew at 8.30. (c) Sorry, I'm supposed to meet my wife at the bus station.

Practice 4

(a) Hold on a minute and I'll put you through. (b) You're wanted on the phone. (c) I've a call for you – will you accept reversed charges? (d) There's no reply. (e) You're supposed to insert a ten-cent coin. (f) Would you replace the receiver? (g) I'll ring you back in a few minutes. (h) Go ahead, caller. (i) Our phone's out of order. (j) You've got the wrong number. (k) We were cut off.

Practice 5

(a) There's no point in looking for the dialling code – there's no automatic dialling in this area. (b) There's no point in holding the line – you're getting the engaged signal. (c) There's no point in putting a coin in – the phone's out of order. (d) There's no point in sending a greetings telegram today – the anniversary's in three weeks' time. (e) There's no point in getting an extension phone – your house is too small.

Practice 6

(a) operator/ can I help you/ fire/ your number/ what exchange/ on/ put you through/ I want to report a fire in the house opposite and the people are away (b) place 2 fingers in the holes directly to the left of the finger stop. Now remove the finger nearest the stop and with your finger in the '9' hole, rotate the dial to the finger stop. Then release your finger and let the dial return. Now place two fingers in the same holes and this time remove the finger furthest from the stop. Rotate the dial twice more to the stop. (c) Just look up the right heading in the telephone directory.

Practice 7

to make some appointments for them/ they'll be writing/ the order for the Geological Institute was despatched on 30 June and they give a waybill number/ us to meet him at the airport on 19 July/ their chairman died on 15 July and the funeral's on the 17th/ to stop payment of a cheque/ he says he'll explain later.

Practice 8

(a) Could I ask you to write 'Fragile – with care' on the outside of the parcel? (b) I'm sorry, but enclosures aren't allowed in an air letter form. (c) I'm sorry, but you can't use the printed paper rate if you've used more than 5 words of greeting. (d) Could I ask you to hand the letter to me and I'll give you a receipt for it.

13

Comprehension questions

(a) Because he had a septic throat. (b) He had a sore throat and a slight fever and it hurt him to swallow. He kept feeling hot and cold and his neck was painful and a bit swollen. (c) He was given an injection and some tablets. (d) He was also told to gargle with warm salt water. (e) When he said, 'It won't hurt me.' (f) The first aid kit. (g) Because she felt faint.

Practice 1

(1) infection (2) patient (3) symptoms (4) sore (5) vomiting (6) insect (7) treatment (8) injection (9) antiseptic

KEY TO PRACTICE EXERCISES   217

Practice 4

'Could you give me some antibiotic tablets for a sore throat?'
'I'm sorry, but you need a prescription for them. What are your symptoms?'
'Well, I've got a slight fever and it hurts me to swallow and my neck's a bit swollen.'
'I think you'd better see a doctor.'

Practice 5

(a) neck (b) sea (c) glass (d) help (e) stitches (f) faint

Practice 6

Cut off a piece of plaster, take a piece of cotton wool and bathe the wound with antiseptic. Take the covering off the plaster and press it on the wound.

Practice 8

(a) read the directions/ dilute it with 5 parts of water/ sip the last dessertspoonful (b) epidemic/ gargling with Sanox night and morning (c) he needs 2 tablets every 2 to 4 hours/ he must chew them and swallow them with water (d) Garadin tablets/ go and see your doctor (e) to dilute it/ your dentist

Practice 9

He was cutting the hedge and then I found him sitting on the ground, so I asked him what was wrong and he said he didn't feel too well. So I rang the hospital and told them what the symptoms were. They sent an ambulance and put him on a stretcher. At the hospital they said they'd admit him and give him some tests and I asked if I could wait. Well, they told me he'd had a heart attack, luckily only a mild one. I asked them if he was going to be all right and they said yes, and that I shouldn't worry. I visited him this morning and he said he felt a lot better. The nurse said he should be well enough to come home by the weekend.

14

Comprehension questions

(a) Because some of the books were damp. (b) For not using enough waterproof paper. (c) Books, posters, photographs and a film. (d) 73.53 (e) To cover the tables. (f) The first caterer's staff had gone on strike. (g) Over 2250 dinars. (h) A folding one. (i) It kept going on and off. (j) No. (k) To get more cloth.

Practice 3

(a) You shouldn't have left those boxes outside. (b) You should've bought six rolls. (c) You should've used more waterproof paper. (d) You should've brought a hammer. (e) You should've telephoned the forwarding agent. (f) You shouldn't have sent the van to my house – you should've sent it to the office. (g) You should've told the workmen to come at six. (h) You shouldn't have left the office door unlocked.

Practice 4

(a) they've/ on strike/ higher wages (b) allow extra time/ the rush-hour (c) using a hammer (d) daresay we can have it in the room marked 'A' (e) you a rough estimate

Practice 5

(a) an office chair, a table, an armchair, shelves, a screen, a cupboard

(b)

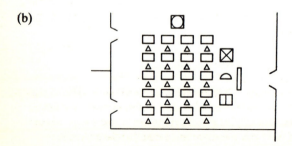

Practice 6

(a) 15 (because he would use 14.78 rolls). (b) plug the fan in/ adjusting the height/ anti-clockwise to loosen it/ clockwise to tighten it/ adjust the angle of fan head/ turn this knob to the left/ press buttons 1 to 3/ pressing button 0

Practice 7

(a) Name: A. M. MASOUD
    Company: Alliance Garages SA
    Address: PO Box 456, Monte Carlo, Monaco.
    Position: General Manager.
(b) (1) forwarding agent (2) cleared (3) loaded (4) van (5) workmen (6) fitted (7) annoyed

15

Comprehension questions

(a) Because the road was up. (b) He couldn't see the back when he was reversing. (c) Because his car broke down. (d) Something was wrong with the engine. (e) By swerving. (f) He reported the accident to the police. (g) None. (h) She was bruised on the arm. (i) She was the only one in the car.

Practice 1

(1) motorway (2) windscreen (3) swerve (4) right-hand (5) turning (6) detour (7) station (8) attendant (9) mechanic (10) replacement (11) litter-bin

Practice 5

(a) really good view (b) no use (c) hang on (d) me a lift/ no room (e) fault was it/ his/ his (f) likely (g) get rid of it/ litter-bin (h) off for lunch/ never mind (i) hand you over to her (j) used to (k) short notice (l) Could you put us up (m) I wish (n) the difference

Practice 6

(a) fine (b) up (c) rucksack (d) drive (e) witnesses (f) injured

Practice 7

(a) there's a camping site at Karun, that's 19 kilometres south of here. (b) Yes, there's one at Musala, that's 95 kilometres south of here and another at Pulan Sa, that's another 102 kilometres further on, but don't forget it's the high season so I suggest you book in advance. (c) so remember that the last filling station before the border is at Marisa but I'm not sure whether they sell premium – there's a shortage of petrol these days. (d) there are only two service stations between here and the border so why don't you have it serviced here in Kemi? (e) I advise you to take the turning almost exactly half-way between Marisa and Rotama (it's marked with a big sign board so you can't miss it) but the road conditions are bad because there's flooding in that area. I think it would be better to go straight on to Pula.

Practice 8

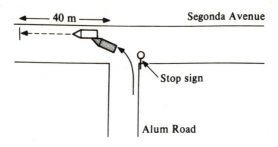

16

Comprehension questions

(a) Directing the traffic. (b) Because the way ahead was blocked and they were in a one-way street. (c) Because his engine stalled. (d) Push his car out of the way. (e) To stop sightseers from getting near the damaged building. (f) Clear away the bricks. (g) To get at someone under the floor beneath the bricks. (h) About getting too near the damaged wall. (i) A leaking gas pipe. (j) The firm which had fitted the pipes. (k) Because the managing director of the firm was talking about legal action.

Practice 4

(a) I doubt whether they'd blow up buildings in the middle of the city. (b) Sorry to bother you but . . . (c) If I were you I'd get your car out of the way. (d) It looks as if we're stuck. (e) Take it easy. (f) Can you manage? (g) Look out. (h) Hey, you. (i) It must have knocked me out. (j) I hope you're better soon. (k) I don't like the sound of that. (l) I've decided against it.

Practice 5

(a) can't help it (b) matter/ fire (c) doesn't matter (d) manage (e) looks as if/ any luck

Practice 6

(a) must have demolished it (b) must have been (c) must have broken (d) must have stalled (e) must have decided

Practice 7

something was wrong/ there were at least 26/ were in a critical condition/ rang the gas company as early as Saturday night/ they didn't bother to check the pipe

Practice 8

(a) I don't remember hearing anything – the thief must have climbed on to the balcony by the fire escape. The balcony door doesn't lock properly and he must have seen my suitcase on the table and my jacket and trousers on the chair. He must have taken them out of the door, which I found open, into the corridor – I doubt whether he was in the room more than 10 seconds. Well, I reported my loss to the manager at ten past six. As well as my clothes, 450 dinars and 1000 US dollars in traveller's cheques were missing.

(b) 'Mr Hall, since the hotel is responsible for the balcony door that didn't lock properly I'm willing to refund your cash.'

'Well, I'm really very grateful.'

'But I suggest you ring the bank to report the loss of your traveller's cheques.'

Practice 9

(1) escape (2) explosion (3) balcony (4) armbands (5) sightseers (6) properly

17

Comprehension questions

(a) Because he said he was sorry to keep them waiting. (b) About getting the blunt scissors. (c) Mr Danby had moved to a new office and had also been on holiday. (d) No – he said 'Come over sometime'. (e) Her mother had been taken ill. (f) He had seen his photograph in the paper recently. (g) No, though he used to. (h) He seemed to be drunk. (i) He kept spilling it. (j) Because he had drunk too much and he had a drink in each hand.

Practice 2

(a) It was very good of you (b) there's no hurry (c) I meant (d) owes you an apology (e) Have you been here long (f) must see about (g) keep

Practice 3

(a) serve him right (b) in charge (c) bet/ must have (d) out of practice

Practice 4

(a) A: very good of you to give me the tickets   B: at all. I hope you/ the way, I'd like to introduce my husband (b) A: I kept you waiting   B: all right, there's no hurry (c) A: what are you doing

KEY TO PRACTICE EXERCISES 223

these days B: to catch up with my painting/ it was very nice to get your invitation/ you must come over for dinner sometime A: Thanks, I'd love to (d) A: Well done! Congratulations on winning B: Well, I guess I was lucky A: think your team will win the cup B: I certainly hope (e) A: excuse me/ had a telephone call to say my brother's been taken ill/ I've got to leave right away B: Very sorry to hear/ it's nothing serious/ know if there's anything I can do A: for inviting me (f) A: May I join you/ the way/ met before/ John Zetta/ head of the music department at Northbank Secondary School B: it must have been at the violin competition last April (g) B: You're joking A: serious/ he says he feels sick B: it serves him right for being so greedy

Practice 5

I'd just like to say a few words. May I say how pleased I am to see such an excellent range of exciting shapes for everything from teacups to television sets and I must congratulate the Arcanian Design Centre on arranging the exhibition so well. I'm certain this exhibition will help to develop trade between Britain and Arcania. Thank you.

Practice 6

(a) reading (b) read (c) ring (d) enjoy (e) doing (f) paper (g) jacket (h) word

Practice 7

(a) A: I'm sorry to bother you/ could you tell me the way to A: would you mind showing me B: must be A: I wonder why (b) A: I suppose B: I'm sure I left it/ do you mind if A: I don't mind/ If you like B: I doubt whether/ needs mending (c) A: What would you like to drink B: I'd rather have A: I'm afraid B: that'll do A: I'll get you/ help yourself. Would you like to (d) A: I daresay there's something wrong B: it looks as if/ so old/ worth repairing A: I see/ supposed to be having B: can't manage that A: that's very kind of you (e) B: try putting A: isn't used to B: would you like me to ring A: you'd better (f) A: put me through to B: at the moment/ hold the line a minute A: don't bother/ have to (g) A: what's the matter/ it's a pity/ instead of B: should've told you first/ anyway/ suggest turning that music down A: how about B: aren't allowed (h) A: excuse me/ anything for removing B: just a minute/ here you are/ to let it dry/ that's right (i) B: we want a lift A: ask him to/ let's ask him if/ find out how much/ that's no use/ how about offering him (j) A: I was sorry to hear about/have you tried feeling/ how about looking/ if I were you/ should contact/ keep looking (k) A: can you manage B: nowhere to sit/ by the way A: I was told/ don't like you/ so as not to/ if you sat/ could smoke

Practice 8

Water!

18

Comprehension questions

(a) The Arcanian Independence Association. (b) It celebrates the end of British rule in Arcania. (c) To build a new road over the Arch. (d) It has formed a committee to discuss the problem. (e) To the Palmville City Council. (f) To leave it where it is, to move it to another site or to demolish it. (g) By taking it to pieces first. (h) They were getting hard to read. (i) To lay a plate on the original site of the Arch. (j) The committee recommended that the Arch should be moved and rebuilt on a suitable new site.

Practice 1

(1) committee (2) Association (3) recommendation (4) proposal (5) Arch (6) Council (7) consider (8) inscription (9) original

Practice 2

(a) feel/ there any chance of persuading them/ none at all, I'm afraid/ this late stage/ must bear in mind that/ after (b) I'd like to ask for your views/ in my opinion (view)/ I don't think we need to

KEY TO PRACTICE EXERCISES 225

worry/ in my opinion (view)/ seems likely that (c) in favour of/ Is there any guarantee that/ must bear in mind that/ or less/ we now come to/ sorry to interrupt, but (d) we've all had time to study/ we've got two alternatives/ all agreed/ could I ask/ my knowledge (e) sum up/ all agreed that/ could I raise/ I suggest (propose)/ a good suggestion/ is everyone in favour? (f) not clear/ it's up to the Council to/ it might be possible to/ much more likely that/ it's a point worth making (g) understand/ the contrary/ other words/ any case/ there's no point in

Practice 3

Mr Alpha: I'd like to ask for your views on investing the pension fund.

Mr Beta: I suggest we put it into shares.

Mr Gamma: Ah, but over the last 18 years shares have only just kept up with inflation and over the last 8 years they haven't even done that. We'd be losing money if we put all of it into shares. So I propose we put some of it into shares and that with the rest we buy some rare stamps or old Gwalian coins.

Mr Alpha: I understand that a lot of people lose money buying and selling stamps. Is there any guarantee that the stamps would rise in value?

Mr Gamma: It might be possible to get advice from my brother – he's a stamp dealer.

Mr Beta: If we bought stamps or coins or pictures we'd have to insure them.

Mr Alpha: Yes, and I wonder if it's difficult to cash them at short notice?

Mr Gamma: There shouldn't be any problem provided we keep in touch with market prices.

ACTIVITIES INDEX

This is a list of the main activities in this book. The numbers refer to the principal Units in which they appear.

Accidents and disasters, dealing with	13, 15, 16
Applications, for visas, jobs	4, 11
Booking journeys	1
Borrowing	3
Changing money	4
Clothes, buying and making	9
Complaining about people and things	3, 5, 9, 17
Customs, getting through	4
Directions, asking the way	2, 5, 8, 15
Eating out	7
Emergencies, dealing with	12, 13, 15, 16
Entertainment, discussing, getting tickets	10
Formal speech and discussion	17, 18
Games, playing	10
Hiring staff	11
— transport (cars, boats)	6
Hotels, staying there and getting things done	5, 6
— talking about reservations	1, 3, 5
Instructions – getting people to do things	10
Insuring	1
Interviewing (for jobs)	11
Invitations	8, 17
Jobs, discussing	11
Lending	3
Losing things	4
Machines, etc., going wrong	3, 11

— operating	15
Manual work – arranging and doing things	5, 11, 14, 18
Ordering drinks, meals	3, 7
Parties, arranging	14, 17
— social behaviour	17
Permission, asking for	1, 2, 3, 4, 17
Post office – sending letters, cables and parcels	12
Reassuring	3, 13
Seats – finding where to sit	3, 17
Shopping	9
Sickness, dealing with	13, 16
Taxis, ordering	5
Telephoning	5, 6, 12
Time off, requesting	11
Tourism – looking at sights	10
Traffic offences, dealing with	8
Travelling by air	1, 2, 3
— bus	4
— car	8, 15, 16
— ship	1, 3
— train	2
Weather – talking about weather and climate	3, 6

IMPORTANT WORDS: A CHECK-LIST

This is a list of the words in the 'boxes'. The numbers refer to the Units in which they first appear. Some of the words may be known to you in other meanings.

A

accompany	4
according to	5
account	1
adhesive tape	12
adjust	14
advance (in –)	5
advisable	6
afford	9
air-conditioned	5
aircraft	3
air hostess	3
airline	1
airmail	6
airport	2
air terminal	1
allergic	13
allowance	2
alternative	18
ambulance	8
amusement	10
anniversary	12
announce	2
annoy	14
antibiotic	13
antiseptic	13
apology	17
applicant	4
application	4
apply (for)	4
appointment	7
arch	18
armband	16
arrangements	5
arrival	3
arrow	2
art gallery	8
article	3
ashore	4
assistant	8
association	8
atmosphere	7
attack (n.)	13
attendant	15
attraction	10
audience	10
authority	12

IMPORTANT WORDS: A CHECK-LIST

automatic	12
available	3
awful	9

B

baggage	1
baggage tag	2
balcony	16
bandage	13
bankrupt	11
bargain (v.)	9
barrier	3
basement	7
bazaar	9
bed (double –)	5
(twin –s)	5
belongings	3
best (do one's –)	5
bill	7
block (n.)	8
block (v.)	15
blow up	16
board (on –)	3
board (v.)	3
boarding card	2
bonnet	15
bonus	11
booking-office	2
border	15
boring	8
bother (v.)	16
branch	8
break down	15
breakdown	15
briefcase	2
brochure	6
business (on –)	1
businessman	4

C

cabin	1
calculator	9
call (at)	4
caller	12
camp(ing) site	15
campus	8
cancel(lation)	1
candidate	11
carburettor	15
cargo	12
carton	3
casual(ly)	6
catch up (with)	17
caterer	14
celebrate	7
certificate	1
change (v.)	1
check in	1
claim (n.)	1
clear (v.)	14
climate	6
clinic	13
clockwise	14
coat hanger	6
cocktail	7
colleague	11
committee	18
complain	5
complimentary	10
compulsory	11
concert	10
conductor	4
confirmation	1
congratulate	17
connection	4
consider	18
contract	11

cottage	5
cotton wool	13
council	18
counter	2
course	7
credit card	5
crew	3
currency	4
custom	6
Customs	3
cut off	12

D

date (out of –)	5
deck	3
declaration	4
declare	4
décor	7
defect (n.)	9
delay (n.)	3
delicious	7
de luxe	5
dentist	13
department store	9
dependant	4
deposit (n.)	5
design (n.)	9
dessert	7
destination	2
detour	15
diagram	18
dial (v.)	5
dialling code	12
dialling tone	12
diarrhoea	13
dilute	13
dimensions	2
direct (adj.)	1

direction	2
directory	12
discount	1
discover	6
disembark	3
dish	7
display (n.)	10
district	8
domestic flight	4
dose (n.)	13
doubtful	15
dress (n.)	10
drink (soft –)	3
driving licence	8
drop (v.)	5
drug (n.)	13
drunk	17
duty free	3

E

earn	11
earphones	3
economy class	1
effects (personal –)	1
electricity	6
embark	3
emergency	12
employ	11
employee	11
employment	4
engaged signal	12
engagement	17
enquiries	16
entertainment	10
equipment	10
essential	6
estimate (n.)	14
exchange (n.)	12

exchange bureau	4
exchange (rate of –)	4
excursion	8
exempt	8
exhibition	1
expenses	1
experience	11
explosion	16
express bus	1
extension	12

F

facilities	5
faint (adj.)	13
fare	1
fasten	3
fault	12
faulty	9
ferry	1
festival	10
fever	13
filing cabinet	14
fill in	3
fine (n. & v.)	8
fire engine	8
fire escape	16
fitting (n.)	9
fix (v.)	14
fixed	9
flask	6
flavour (v.)	7
flooding	15
fluent	11
flush (v.)	5
flyover	8
folk	10
forecast (n.)	15
foreigner	4
foreman	11
forwarding agent	14
fragile	12
frontier	4
funds	18

G

gangway	3
gargle	13
get off	4
get on	13
get through	12
give up	11
goods	9
graduate (n.)	11
grateful	9
greedy	17
greetings	12
guide	8
guidebook	3

H

hand baggage	2
handicraft	10
harbour	3
harvest	10
headache	13
heading	12
headquarters	8
help oneself	7
hire	3
hire-purchase	9
hitchhiker	15
hold on (to)	10
home-made	7
horrible	13
hospitality	7

host	17
humid	6
hurry (in a –)	7
hydrofoil	1

I

immigration	3
import (v.)	4
infection	13
initial (n.)	4
injection	13
inscription	18
insect	13
insist (on)	11
insurance	1
interrupt	18
interval	10
interview (n. & v.)	11
introduce	17
invalid (n.)	3
invitation card	8
issue (v.)	4

J

join in	10
joke (v.)	17

L

land (v.)	3
landing card	3
lane	8
let go (of)	10
librarian	8
lifejacket	3
lightweight	6
liquid	13
litter-bin	15
load (v.)	14
located	7

M

machinery	11
maid	5
maintain	6
malaria	13
manage	5
management	5
match (n.)	10
maximum	1
measurements	9
mechanic	15
medical	1
medicine	3
member(ship)	6
menswear	9
menu	7
meter	5
mild	13
mileage	6
minimum	5
missing	4
monsoon	6
monument	18
mood	17
mosquito	13
motel	15
museum	8

N

night club	5
non-smoking section	2
nurse	13

O

obligation	9
offence	8
official (n.)	2
ointment	13
old-fashioned	9
one-way street	8
operator	12
orchestra	10
order (out of –)	12
original	18
outskirts	8
overlook	7
overseas	6
overtake	8
overtime	11
overweight	2
owner	8

P

painful	13
panel	14
parallel	8
park(ing)	2
part-exchange (n. & v.)	9
part-time	11
passage	2
passenger	2
passport control	2
patient (n.)	13
pattern	9
pedestrian crossing	8
pension	11
performance	10
period	13
permanent	11
petrol station	15
pick up	5
picnic	6
pie	7
pieces (come to –)	9
(take to –)	9
pilot	3
pity (n.)	10
plaster	13
platform	2
plug in	14
point (n.)	10
portable	3
post (n.)	11
poster	10
pottery	10
powder	13
power cut	6
pregnant	11
premium	1
prescription	13
preserve (v.)	18
press (n.)	11
press (v.)	6
pretty (adv.)	7
procession	10
product	9
programme	10
prohibited	3
properly	16
proposal	18
public holiday	3
public transport	4
pushchair	2
put off	4
put right	12
put through	12
put up	15

Q

qualification(s)	11
qualified	11
quality	9
quay	3
queue (n.)	2
quotation	6

R

rainfall	6
range (n.)	17
rate	5
receipt	1
receiver	12
reception	5
recipe	7
recommendation	18
reference(s)	11
refreshment lounge	2
refund (n.)	3
register (v.)	12
replacement	14
republic	18
rescue	12
reservation	1
responsible	17
restoration	18
retired	17
reverse (v.)	15
reversed charges	12
right-hand drive	8
roll (n.)	14
roof rack	5
rough	6
route	2
row (n.)	3
rucksack	15
rude	17
run out (of)	9
rush-hour	2

S

salary	8
salesman	6
satisfied	9
scale (n.)	8
scenery	15
score (n. & v.)	10
screen (n.)	14
sea front	16
seal (v.)	12
seat belt	3
second-hand	9
secretary	8
security check	3
see out	17
selection	7
septic	13
serve	7
service	3
set off	15
settle up	7
shape (v.)	9
shellfish	7
shift (n.)	11
short cut	6
short of	6
shoulder bag	2
show (n.)	10
sightseer16	16
sign board	2
skill	11
slip (n.)	4
snack bar	7
socket	5

sold out	9
solution	13
sort out	5
souvenir	9
spare (adj.)	9
spectator	10
speed limit	8
stadium	8
staff	8
stall (v.)	16
statue	8
steward(ess)	3
sting (n.)	13
stitch (n.)	13
storage compartment	3
stretcher	13
style	9
suburbs	8
suggest	7
suit (v.)	9
suitable	6
suite	5
superb	7
supermarket	6
surgery	13
swallow	13
swerve	15
swimming costume	6
switch on	3
swollen	13
symbol	14
symptom	13

T

tablet	13
take-off (n.)	3
take off (v.)	3
tape recorder	3
tariff	5
tarmac	15
taxi rank	3
team	10
telex	6
temperature	3
temporary	11
tennis court	10
terrific	16
time (in –)	2
(on –)	3
timetable	1
tourist	4
traditional	10
traffic jam	2
traffic lights	8
transfer	12
transit	3
travel agency	1
traveller's cheque	4
treatment	13
trip	2
trolley (luggage –)	2
tropical	7
trunk call	12
try on	9
tunnel	18
turning	8
turnstile	3
tyre	15

U

underground railway	2
underpass	8
unmade road	15
unpack	6
used (adj.)	15
U-turn	8

V

vacancy	11
vacation	11
valid	1
value (n. & v.)	9
van	14
vehicle	8
view (n.)	15
visa	4
vomit(ing)	13
voucher	1

W

wallet	8
washable	6
waterproof	14
weigh	2
windscreen	15
witness (n.)	15
workman	14
wrap up	9